OLD NORSE MADE NEW

ESSAYS ON THE POST-MEDIEVAL RECEPTION
OF OLD NORSE LITERATURE AND CULTURE

EDITED BY
DAVID CLARK AND CARL PHELPSTEAD

VIKING SOCIETY FOR NORTHERN RESEARCH
UNIVERSITY COLLEGE LONDON
2007

© Viking Society for Northern Research 2007

Printed by Short Run Press Limited, Exeter

ISBN: 978-0-903521-76-5

Repritned 2018

The printing of this book is made possible by a gift to the University of Cambridge in memory of Dorothea Coke, Skjaeret, 1951.

Front cover: 'A Funeral of a Viking' by Francis Dicksee (1893),
© Manchester Art Gallery, reproduced with permission.

CONTENTS

Preface

Foreword — ANDREW WAWN — v

Thomas Gray's Translations of Old Norse Poetry — ALISON FINLAY — 1

Translating the *Poetic Edda* into English — CAROLYNE LARRINGTON — 21

William Morris and the Volsungs — DAVID ASHURST — 43

In Search of the Lakeland Saga: Antiquarian Fiction and the Norse Settlement in Cumbria — MATTHEW TOWNEND — 63

Tolkien and Old Norse Antiquity: Real and Romantic Links in Material Culture — DIMITRA FIMI — 83

From Runic Inscriptions to Runic Gymnastics — HEATHER O'DONOGHUE — 101

A Viking Pacifist? The Life of St Magnus in Saga, Novel, and Opera — CARL PHELPSTEAD — 119

Old Norse Made New: Past and Present in Modern Children's Literature — DAVID CLARK — 133

PREFACE

Earlier versions of most of the essays in this collection were delivered at the Viking Society Student Conference on the theme of 'Old Norse Made New' held at the University of Oxford on 25 February 2006 (Clark, Fimi, Finlay, O'Donoghue, Phelpstead, and Townend). Following the conference it was felt that the papers could be published alongside others on medievalist topics from previous Viking Society Student Conferences (Ashurst and Larrington). We hope that the resulting volume will appeal to students and others with an interest in the ways in which Old Norse literature and the medieval culture of Iceland and Scandinavia have influenced writers, especially writers in English, after the Middle Ages. In recent years the study of medievalism, the post-medieval reception and influence of medieval literature and culture, has become an increasingly productive field of research as scholars have realized that interrogating past constructions of the medieval is a valuable way of reflecting on their own relationship to the material they study. The essays collected here cover a wide chronological span (from the eighteenth century to the twenty-first) and a range of literary genres (poetry, novel, libretto, children's literature, fantasy fiction); we very much hope that the variety of subject matter examined in this collection will inspire others to pursue further research in this rich field.

We would like to thank the organizers of the Oxford conference, Carolyne Larrington and Heather O'Donoghue, for encouraging us to edit the papers for publication. We are also grateful to Alison Finlay for overseeing the production of the book and join her in thanking Anthony Faulkes and Peter Forshaw for technical assistance with the illustrations. We must also thank Andrew Wawn, not only for contributing a characteristically bracing Foreword to the collection, but also for generously casting an expert eye over the essays. Publication of the volume has been assisted by a substantial grant from the Dorothea Coke Fund.

We are grateful to the following for permission to reproduce copyright illustrations: Manchester Art Gallery for 'A Funeral of a Viking' by Francis Dicksee (front cover); the Tolkien Estate, HarperCollins Publishers Ltd., and Houghton Mifflin Company for J. R. R. Tolkien's sketch of the Crown of Gondor (fig. 5); the Tolkien Estate and the Bodleian Library, Oxford, for Tolkien's drawing of the Winged Crown of Gondor (fig. 8); and Kevin Brown for his drawing of the Crowns of Egypt (fig. 4).

David Clark
Carl Phelpstead

FOREWORD

ANDREW WAWN

The trail of links and implications from three little-known books may serve to launch this collection of essays on making Old Norse and the old north new. All three volumes were written in the 1920s by the same author, who was born in Adel, in north-west Leeds, within a stone's throw of where the present writer now lives. The author's father, Octavius (no less!), was a prominent civic figure and stalwart of the local Philosophical and Literary Society, and the author himself was Ernest Rücker Eddison (1882–1945). In Eddison's three volumes, two novels and a translation, we may observe many of the processes and priorities of the old northern medievalism explored in the present volume.

The first novel, *The Worm Ouroboros* (1922), begins with a scene set in North Yorkshire: it is evening in a country house in Wastdale in the 1920s, and a middle-aged couple have just finished dinner; while their daughter plays the spinet in the next room the wife has a suggestion for post-prandial entertainment—'Should we finish that chapter of *Njal's saga*?' And that is just what they do. She reads the saga chapter out loud from the household copy with its faded green cover—a detail that identifies it as the celebrated *Story of Burnt Njal* (1861) translation of *Njáls saga* done by the accomplished Victorian Icelandicist George Webbe Dasent. The chapter, accurately quoted in the novel, describes one of the portents that preceded the burning of Njáll and his family at Bergþórshváll. Hildiglúmr Runólfsson sees a man on horseback bearing a burning brand; after singing a verse about Flosi and fire the man hurls the brand at the mountains, which are duly set ablaze; he then disappears—and soon afterwards Njáll and his family are burnt to death. Our Wastdale couple finish the chapter and retire to bed, only for the sleeping husband to have a vision even more disturbing than that of Hildiglúmr. The remainder of the novel describes that vision. We read of conflict between two mighty cosmic forces, and of a vulnerable young hero and his friend compelled to undertake epic journeys; on the way they encounter wizards, dwarfs, and goblins; there are magic spells, swords and cloaks, aged kings, councils of war, and a ring of symbolic importance. The story is told in archaized language, and there are Old English, Old Icelandic (and William Morrisean) echoes in the landscapes and nomenclature, as, for example, with references to Trentmar from 'Scorradale'.

'Skorradale' appears in the second Eddison book to which I draw attention. It can be found on a map accompanying his *Egil's saga; done into English out of the Icelandic with an introduction, notes, and an essay on some principles of translation* (1930). As the sub-title suggests, this is no broad-brush version of the saga by a blundering amateur. Published by Cambridge University Press, the painstakingly accurate text is accompanied by thoughtful annotation that acknowledges the assistance received from major scholars in the field, among them Bertha Phillpotts (Eddison's Cambridge contact), Sigurður Nordal, Finnur Jónsson, and Bogi Ólafsson, a teacher of English at the Menntaskóli in Reykjavík. The preface and notes also confirm that Eddison, like many Victorian enthusiasts before him, had visited the saga-steads of Borgarfjörður, and was proud of the fact. He had stayed at the district school at Hvanneyri, just south of Borg, and dedicates the volume to his Anglophile hostess Svava Þórhallsdóttir. It may be that Eddison shared an interest in the kind of visionary spiritualism reflected in her published Icelandic translations of several such English works.

Alongside the 1922 fantasy novel and 1930 saga translation stands Eddison's historical novel *Styrbiorn the Strong* (1926). By the 1920s novelistic versions of Old Icelandic sagas were nothing new—in English that trail had already been blazed in works about heroes such as Grettir Ásmundarson, Leifr Eiríksson and, latterly, Gísli Súrsson, courtesy of Maurice Hewlett's *The Outlaw* (1924). The eponymous hero of Eddison's narrative was a less familiar figure. Styrbjörn, nephew and ward of King Eirekr of Sweden, who eventually challenged his uncle for the throne at the battle of Fýrisvellir, is mentioned briefly in a handful of sagas, and more extensively in *Styrbjarnar þáttr Svíakappa* (*Flateyjarbók*, ed. Sigurður Nordal 1945 II 146–49). Only a serious and imaginative Icelandicist would have had the wit to make such a figure the subject of a novel, and the knowledge to flesh out his tale with material from other sagas, and the confidence to narrate the tale so deftly.

Three books, then, by the same author, and if we add up his score we find an Oxford graduate with a not very English-sounding middle name, who had lived in Leeds, was an accomplished Icelandicist, was known to learned Icelanders, and had authored an heroic fantasy novel with a strong Icelandic and Old English inflection. This could almost be a pen-portrait of J. R. R. Tolkien. The two men seem never to have met in Leeds during Tolkien's tour of duty as Reader in English Language at the university 1920–24, and Professor 1924–25. However, their paths did eventually cross on at least one occasion in Oxford during the war, Eddison by this time having moved to London, where he spent much of his later life as a senior civil servant.

The medievalist template established by Eddison's three publications involves a well-informed philological awareness, an instinctive regionalism, an unrelenting commitment to outreach through translation and novelistic recreation (both historical and futuristic), and a wide-ranging engagement with Old Icelandic poetry and prose (not least the visions in *Njáls saga*). It is the exploration of just such elements that lies at the heart of the essays in *Old Norse Made New*. We learn of Thomas Gray's engagement with the supernatural in *Njáls saga*; of the traditions of translating eddic verse from 1797 to the present day; of the style and substance of Morris' poetry and Tolkien's prose; of regional fictions set in the Lake district and in Orkney; and of old northern voices and values in modern children's literature. It is, in truth, hard to imagine Eddison taking part in runic gymnastics, but it would not be difficult to identify a cultural politics (albeit one less sulphurous than that of Guido von List and his admirers) underpinning his medievalism.

Eddison seems not to have been a member of the Viking Society, but there is every reason to believe that he would have relished the medievalist witness represented by the essays in this volume published under the Society's imprint. The editors and the present author hope that these papers will also find favour with present-day readers eager to explore the ways in which dedicated British enthusiasts over several centuries have sought to make Old Norse and the old north their own.

THOMAS GRAY'S TRANSLATIONS OF OLD NORSE POETRY

ALISON FINLAY

According to a legend of the early nineteenth century General Wolfe, who captured Quebec from the French in 1759, carried into the battle a copy of Thomas Gray's 'Elegy Written in a Country Church Yard'. The night before the battle he reputedly read the poem aloud to his officers, saying, 'I would rather have been the author of that piece than beat the French tomorrow.'[1] To the reader of Old Norse literature this story irresistibly suggests a parallel with the story of St Óláfr, before the Battle of Stiklastaðir in 1030, calling on his Icelandic poet Þormóðr Kolbrúnarskáld to recite the *Bjarkamál*, a heroic lay calling on legends from the heroic Danish past in order to awaken the warriors to battle.[2] Both stories are likely to be apocryphal, but the parallel serves as a reminder that the poetry of the eighteenth century, even in a meditative vein, had a public, generalizing function not dissimilar to that of the works produced by the Old Norse court skalds. The awakening appetite for the 'Gothic' that Gray was among the first to exploit marks a new preoccupation with the response of the reader, in terms of the evocation of emotions such as fear and horror, that delves below the smooth surface of eighteenth-century poetic decorum.

Gray's 'Elegy' was published in 1751 and won instant success as the iconic poem of its age: meditative, reflective, expressing a sense of mourning as its title implies, but in a generalized, abstracted vein characteristic of the public voice of eighteenth-century poetry. There may be a foretaste of the empathy of later romantic poets for the simple and rustic in the lamentation for the unsung lives of the 'Rude forefathers of the Hamlet', but this is broadened into the eternal philosophical proposition that the rewards of pomp and riches are fleeting (Gray 1966, 38):

> Let not Ambition mock their useful toil,
> Their homely joys, and destiny obscure;
> Nor Grandeur hear with a disdainful smile,
> The short and simple annals of the Poor.

---

[1] For an examination of the legend, see Stokes 1929, 83–88.

[2] The story is told in *Óláfs saga helga* in *Heimskringla* (Snorri Sturluson 1941–51, II 361–62).

> The boast of heraldry, the pomp of pow'r,
> And all that beauty, all that wealth e'er gave,
> Awaits alike th' inevitable hour.
> The paths of glory lead but to the grave.

The harmonious, balanced manipulation of metre and rhyme and the Latinate diction conform to the principles of classical decorum that prevailed in Gray's time. The poem was enormously influential: more than fifty separate editions were published in the first fifty years after its composition, leaving aside its countless appearances in periodicals and anthologies, where indeed it has featured as a staple ever since.

Gray's two translations, or imitations as he called them himself, of Old Norse poems were also influential, but in a different direction. Written before 1761, though not published till 1768, they mark the beginning of the taste for the supernatural, craggy, and mysterious that became a strong fashion at the end of the eighteenth century and sought its narratives and conceptual schemes from cultures other than the classical Latin and Greek models that had held sway for the past century. It is this fashion for the dark and dramatic that leads the heroine of *Northanger Abbey* to startle her social circle with the announcement (Austen 1933, V 112),

> I have heard that something very shocking indeed, will soon come out in London. [...] I have [...] heard that it is to be more horrible than any thing we have met with yet. [...] It is to be uncommonly dreadful. I shall expect murder and every thing of the kind.

Jane Austen, writing in the 1790s, was mocking the current fad for fantastic horror fiction, the Gothic novel; to Catherine Morland, 'horrible' and 'uncommonly dreadful' are terms of high praise. In fact the term 'Gothic' for this style of fiction harks back to the customary reference, in Gray's time, to the Germanic or Teutonic as 'Gothic'. This can be seen in Gray's note at the beginning of 'The Fatal Sisters', explaining the meaning of 'valkyrie' (Gray 1966, 214):

> *Note*—The *Valkyriur* were female Divinities, Servants of *Odin* (or *Woden*) in the Gothic mythology: their name signifies *Chuser[s] of the slain*. They were mounted on swift horses with drawn swords in their hands, & in the throng of battle selected such as were destined to slaughter, & conducted them to *Valhalla*, the hall of *Odin*, or paradise of the Brave, where they attended the banquet, & served the departed Heroes with horns of mead & ale.

The selection of poems that Gray chose to translate is, at first sight, surprising. 'The Fatal Sisters' is a version of *Darraðarljóð*, a poem loosely classified as skaldic although its metre is the eddic *fornyrðislag*. It is found in chapter 157 of *Njáls saga* in the context of the saga's narrative of the battle of Clontarf, where it is supposedly chanted by a group of supernatural females—identified by Gray as valkyries, as the poem itself hints but does not state explicitly—who are depicted before the battle weaving a cloth from the intestines of dead warriors, on a loom weighted with human heads. The second poem, 'The Descent of Odin', is based on *Baldrs draumar* (called *Vegtamskviða* in some of the manuscripts where it is preserved), a mythological poem of eddic type although it is not actually found in the Codex Regius collection. It narrates Óðinn's descent into the underworld to interrogate a *vǫlva* (Gray's translation is 'Prophetess') from the world of the dead, about the fate in store for his dead son Baldr. From a modern point of view the choice seems obscure, largely because both poems fall outside the generic and editorial categories imposed by modern scholarship: *Darraðarljóð* as a poem neither fully eddic nor metrically skaldic, divorced from the mythical and legendary narrative cycles of the *Poetic Edda* and peripheral to the main narrative of the saga text in which it survives, and *Baldrs draumar* as part of the 'Eddica minora', the poems relevant to the cycle found in the Codex Regius but not actually included in it.

Gray's choice needs to be seen in context, not only that of the limited access that he had to Old Norse texts, but also the nature of the project in which he originally intended to incorporate his translations. The 'advertisement' preceding these texts (together with a third poem, 'The Triumphs of Owen') in the 1768 edition of his poems, in which they were first published, outlines this (Gray 1966, 27):

> The Author once had thoughts (in concert with a friend) of giving *the History of English Poetry*: In the Introduction to it he meant to have produced some specimens of the Style that reigned in ancient times among the neighbouring nations, or those who had subdued the greater part of this Island, and were our Progenitors: the following three Imitations made a part of them. He has long since drop'd his design, especially after he had heard, that it was already in the hands of a Person well qualified to do it justice, both by his taste, and his researches into antiquity.[3]

The person of taste referred to is Thomas Warton, Professor of Poetry at Oxford from 1756 to 1766 (Lonsdale 1969, 210–14, Clunies Ross 1998, 24). His *History of English Poetry* appeared in 1774, without

---

[3] A facsimile of the page can be viewed at <http://www.thomasgray.org/cgi-bin/view.cgi?collection=primary&edition=1768>, p. 75.

the Norse (or indeed Celtic or Anglo-Saxon) material originally included in Gray's scheme, though Warton makes some informed remarks about skaldic diction (Warton 1774; but see Clunies Ross 1998, 47–50). Gray's mooted history was planned in collaboration with his friend William Mason. Warton's competing history may have served as a convenient excuse for its abandonment, but Gray notoriously failed to finish projects, as he acknowledged in a letter to his friend Horace Walpole when he sent him a copy of his 'Elegy': 'You will, I hope, look upon it in the light of a *thing with an end to it*; a merit that most of my writings have wanted, and are like to want'.[4] The 'advertisement' underlines Gray's scholarly attitude to his material, but more significantly, the fact that he was staking a claim to the products of Viking culture as a close extension of the English: 'those who had subdued the greater part of this Island, and were our Progenitors'. In this context it may be significant that he gives as source for 'The Fatal Sisters' 'the *Orcades* of Thormodus Torfaeus. Hafniæ. 1697', only then adding '& also in Bartholinus' (Gray 1966, 29), a reference to the work of Thomas Bartholin, which was in fact Torfaeus's source. The Orcadian relevance of *Darraðarljóð* perhaps gave it a particular priority for Gray and caused him to cite this more specifically Orcadian source. Also to be noted is the equivalence in Gray's mind, and that of his contemporaries, of early Scandinavian and Celtic cultures. Margaret Omberg (1976, 26) notes that the Ossianic poems of James Macpherson, published in 1762 and 1763 and much admired by Gray, not only stoked the enthusiasm of the eighteenth-century literary world for the exotic charms of primitive poetry in general, but were also

> instrumental in the awakening of interest in ancient Scandinavia. Their inspirational effect on both Gray and Percy suggests that without this initial stimulus, Gray would not have written his Norse odes, nor Percy produced his translations of northern poetry in *Five Pieces of Runic Poetry*.

Among the settings of the Ossianic poems is Inistore, that is, Orkney, at the time of Viking rule, and the Scandinavians feature as the traditional enemies of the Celtic protagonists—precisely the setting that forms the backdrop to 'The Fatal Sisters'. Macpherson's attempts to differentiate Celtic and Viking cultures are at best superficial, though Omberg argues that Macpherson's dependence on information gleaned from Mallet's *Introduction à l'histoire de Dannemarc* increased in the course of his writing (Omberg 1976, 30). The fact that the third 'specimen' of

---

[4] June 12, 1750 (Toynbee and Whibley [1935] 1971, I 327); see also Walpole's remark cited in Note 13 below.

early poetry carried over by Gray from the aborted History to the 1768 edition of his poems was the Welsh 'The Triumphs of Owen' supports the view that Gray did not strongly differentiate the Norse from the Celtic, although Margaret Clunies Ross (1998, 106) gives him credit for a scholarly discrimination beyond that of many contemporaries:

> His Commonplace Books reveal that he read very widely indeed in available seventeenth- and eighteenth-century Scandinavian authors, and was not taken in by fashionable hypotheses or confusions such as the Celtic/Teutonic one perpetrated by Mallet.

Gray's access to Old Norse texts was mediated through the works of antiquarians writing in Latin, but his Commonplace Books confirm the wide range of his reading in the available material. A considerable amount of antiquarian literature was available, going back as early as the Danish Ole Worm, whose *Runer seu Danica literatura antiquissima* was published in 1636, and, in England, the works of William Temple (1690) and George Hickes (1705). More recently, in 1755 the Swiss writer Mallet's *Introduction à l'Histoire de Dannemarc* reached a wider audience, and was enthusiastically read by Gray. Some of these works were rare, but that was no problem for Gray who led a reclusive life in Cambridge as a fellow of Peterhouse, moving to Pembroke College when Peterhouse became too rowdy. When in 1759 he moved to London, he immediately retreated into the newly opened British Museum. So he was well placed for access to scholarly collections. There is scholarly precision, too, in Gray's citing of his source at the beginning of each Ode. As already noted, the 'The Fatal Sisters' is attributed to Thormodus Torfaeus, the Latinized name of the Icelandic scholar Þormóðr Torfason, who quoted *Darraðarljóð* in the preface to his history of Orkney (1697). Gray acknowledges the presence of the poem also in 'Bartholinus', who is also named as the source for 'The Descent of Odin'.

The Danish scholar Bartholin's *Antiquitatum Danicarum de causis contemptæ a Danis adhuc gentilibus mortis* was published, also in Copenhagen, in 1689. This work was highly influential, not only because of its many citations of Old Norse poetry and sagas, together with Latin translations, which were a mine for authors like Gray, but also in terms of the contextual framework in which they were set. Bartholin, who held the position of Antiquarius Regius—official antiquary to the Danish Crown—had as his amanuensis and assistant the famous Icelandic scholar and manuscript collector Árni Magnússon, who provided him with the Icelandic texts and translations for his work (Már Jónsson

1998, 37–40). Bartholin's argument is suggested by the title of his treatise, which can be translated as 'Danish antiquities concerning the causes of the Danes' contempt for death while they were still pagan'. He aimed to represent the ancient Danes, by which he meant the Scandinavian peoples in general, as stoical heroes whose indifference to bodily pain and belief in an afterlife had something in common with Christianity, despite their pagan status. Margaret Clunies Ross summarizes the thesis (1998, 83):

> Whereas the Romans died for their republic, the Danes, obeying their kings, chose to die in battle rather than in bed. The Danes also had a horror of being taken as captives of war and they scorned the pain of torture. The moral imperative of dying an honourable and glorious death was thus a strong impulse to extraordinary courage. The other major reason why the Danes scorned death derived from their religious beliefs in the survival of the soul, particularly the warrior soul which was held to travel straight to Valhalla.

We see here the origin of the stereotype of the Nordic hero who laughs in the face of death, which has exercised a powerful influence on English-speaking enthusiasts for Old Norse literature ever since. Bartholin illustrated his claim using a wide range of 'old codices and monuments until now unedited',[5] including laws, historical texts, and sagas as well as poetry, sometimes whole poems and sometimes single stanzas quoted as illustration to the argument. Since many of these texts had indeed not been published before, the range of Old Norse literature available to the scholarly world was greatly enlarged.

Gray's choice of material for his two Odes, then, should be seen against the background of the access to Old Norse literature afforded to him in this generous anthology. The Commonplace Book in which he wrote notes for these two poems, as well as the Latin texts from which he translated them and, ultimately, drafts of the poems themselves, also includes, as it happens, the fragmentary *Bjarkamál* mentioned above.[6] Gray found this too in Bartholin, for whose thesis it provides ample support. An earlier Commonplace Book contains a list of poems, including those on which Gray based his Odes, under the heading

---

[5] This translates the book's sub-title, 'ex vetustis codicibus & monumentis hactenus ineditis congesti' (Clunies Ross 1998, 83).

[6] The Latin versions of *Baldrs draumar*, *Darraðarljóð*, and the *Bjarkamál* fragment are transcribed in Gray's *Commonplace Book*, III 1041–47; his autograph texts of 'The Fatal Sisters' and 'The Descent of Odin' appear on pp. 1068 and 1070 (Clunies Ross 1998, 106).

'Gothic',[7] noting his sources for each. Omberg (1976, 39) reproduces the list with the speculation that it was 'presumably intended as a guide for translations to be included in the projected history of English poetry':

Incantation of Woden's (call'd Vegtams Kvitha) very ancient. in Bartholin p. 632.
    Destroyed by Hella, in Ireland
Death Song of Regner Lodbrog, King of Denmark. About in Mallet and Wormius.
A.D. 859.
    Hardraade
Harald the Brave, Prince of Norway's Complaint of the
cruelty of his Mistress Elissif, Daughter of Jarislas,
King of Russia, middle of the 11th Century *(from the Olafs
Noregs Konunga)* in Mallet and Barthol.
The Praises of Haquin, slain in battle in 960, and Ode
written by Eyvind, Chief of the Skalds, Cousin to this
Prince, who was son of Harald Harfax, First King of all
Norway in Mallet.
Some parts of the Voluspa (cited so often in the Edda)
or Oracles of Vola & the Havamaal, or Sublime Discourse
of Woden, preserved by Saemund Sigfusson (in
the first Edda) who was born in 1057. In Mallet and Resenius.
The song of the Weird Sisters, or Valkyries—
after A.D. 1029 In Tormodus Torfaeus, Orcad.
    & Bartholin.
Dialogue of Hervor and Angantyr In Peringskiold and Dr. Hickes.

The list shows the wide range, within the limits of his time and its Latinate culture, of Gray's reading, and a fairly eclectic choice of sources: poems both eddic and skaldic, including praise poems, elegies, and love songs, as well as the elements of incantation and 'sublime discourse', ranging in date from 'very ancient' to 'after A.D. 1029' (though not strictly in chronological order, since the latter is followed by the 'ancient' *Waking of Angantýr*).

In the absence of other evidence as to why the two extant lays were the first (and apparently only) adaptations actually undertaken by Gray, we may deduce that what attracted him about these two poems was their setting in a liminal space between the human and the supernatural or between life and death, and their use of strong visual images. Gray's practice in his versions is to emphasize and expand the representation of

---

[7] At the beginning of *Commonplace Book* II. A second list of Anglo-Saxon and Celtic pieces follows. The italics are Omberg's and indicate Gray's later annotations to the list.

these images, while keeping to a minimum any sense of their belonging to a wider context: the fact that their mythological background was unfamiliar to the reader adds to their mysterious power.

The reliance of the poems on dramatic visual images evidently contributed to their wide appeal and was picked up by two contemporary visual artists who contributed strongly to the Gothic movement: William Blake and the Swiss Henry Fuseli, who both illustrated 'The Descent of Odin'; Blake made ten watercolours of this and another ten of 'The Fatal Sisters' as part of a set of illustrations to Gray's collected poems, executed between 1797 and 1798. The earliest sketch for Fuseli's 'Odin in the Underworld' can be dated to 1771, and is therefore a very early response to Gray's poem.[8]

Gray, then, was in the vanguard of the search for new and striking images, which often in fact took the form of the old and primitive, His aim was to regenerate the rigid conventions of eighteenth-century classicism with a new interest in the sublime. At the same time Gray makes no attempt to cut loose from the harmonious and regular form and diction that characterized his 'Elegy'. He was an accomplished classicist who composed more verse in Latin than in English, and was strongly opposed to the view later proposed by Wordsworth in his Preface to *Lyrical Ballads* (Coleridge and Wordsworth 1802, vii) that the language of poetry should be 'language really used by men'. Gray was happy to assert the opposite:[9]

> The language of the age is never the language of poetry [. . .]. Our poetry [. . .] has a language peculiar to itself; to which almost every one, that has written, has added something by enriching it with foreign idioms and derivatives: Nay sometimes words of their own composition or invention. Shakespear and Milton have been great creators this way; and no one more licentious than Pope or Dryden, who perpetually borrow expressions from the former.

His Norse poems maintain this elevated diction, not only in the choice of Latinate terms—of blood, for example, the words 'gore', 'carnage', 'ensanguined', and 'crimson' are used—but in phrases borrowed from poets such as Shakespeare, Milton, and Spenser. These he actually emphasizes by pointing out the parallels in footnotes: in 'The Fatal

---

[8] These and other illustrations of Gray's works are analysed by Margaret Clunies Ross (1998, 118–66), including reproductions in black and white. Blake's paintings can be viewed in colour at <http://www.blakearchive.org> (go to 'Works in the archive', then 'Illustrations to Gray's "Poems" (c. 1797–98)').

[9] Letter to Richard West, April 1742 (Toynbee and Whibley [1935] 1971, I 192).

Sisters', following the explanatory note on valkyries, Gray has two notes referring to echoes from *Paradise Lost* and *Julius Caesar*; and the influence on this poem of *Macbeth* has frequently been noted (Clunies Ross 1998, 117). Blake, incidentally, replaces the twelve 'sisters' of Gray's poem (which accurately follows its Norse source in this respect) with three, aligning them with the three 'weird sisters' in *Macbeth* but also with the classical belief in three Fates. As Clunies Ross points out (1998, 118),

> these overt canonical references [. . .] embedded this new poetry with its exotic subject matter in an accepted imaginative context and allowed [the reader] to feel secure in the minor adventure of discovering that the antique Norse sublime [. . .] was not too different from Shakespeare, Milton and the classics.

The exploration of unfamiliar and primitive cultures and the emphasis on the supernatural and terrible was characteristic of the eighteenth-century quest for the sublime in both visual and literary forms. As it was described by theorists of the time, the objective was to shock the imagination into the abandonment of the reflective mode, so that the distinction between the object being described and its representation is elided:[10]

> and the brain being deeply penetrated by those impressions, the very objects themselves are set as it were before us, and consequently we are sensible of the same passion that we should feel from the things themselves [. . .]; and therefore when the imagination is so inflamed, as to render the soul utterly incapable of reflecting, there is no difference between the images and the things themselves.

In *A Philosophical Enquiry into the Origin of our Ideas of the Sublime and Beautiful*, published in 1757, Edmund Burke argued that 'terror' was 'in all cases whatsoever [. . .] the ruling principle of the sublime', elaborating the psychological mechanism by which this aesthetic principle was perceived to operate on the receiver (Burke 1757, I vii: 13):

> Whatever is fitted in any sort to excite the ideas of pain, and danger, that is to say, whatever is in any sort terrible, or is conversant about terrible objects, or operates in a manner analogous to terror, is a source of the *sublime*; that is, it is productive of the strongest emotion which the mind is capable of feeling.

Terror, then, is thought of as a trigger, that shocks the reader's mind into a powerful emotional engagement with the work. Gray himself wrote to his Scottish publisher Beattie that he was attracted by the 'wild spirit' of

---

[10] John Dennis, writing in 1704 of Homer and Virgil (cited in Clunies Ross 1998, 108).

these poems,[11] and many readers responded in similar terms, Beattie stating approvingly in reply that[12]

> The *Fatal Sisters* exhibits a collection of the most frightful images that ever occupied human imagination: some of them in the hands of an ordinary Poet would have sunk into burlesque (particularly the circumstance of the warriors heads) but You have made every thing magical and dreadful; Your choice of words on this, as on every other occasion, is the happiest that can be.

Such enthusiasm was not universal. Gray's friend Horace Walpole, himself an early proponent of the Gothic whose novel, *The Castle of Otranto*, was published in 1767, commented that 'Gray has translated two noble incantations from the Lord knows who, a Danish Gray, who lived the Lord knows when',[13] and still more dismissively,[14]

> Gray has added to his poems three ancient Odes from Norway and Wales. The subjects of the two first are grand and picturesque, and there is his genuine vein in them; but they are not interesting, and do not, like his other poems, touch any passion. Our human passions, which he masters at will in his former pieces, are here not affected. Who can care through what horrors a Runic savage arrived at all the joys and glories they could conceive, the supreme felicity of boozing ale out of the skull of an enemy in Odin's Hall?

It is interesting that Walpole reproduces, and by implication attributes quite unfairly to Gray, the ubiquitous misconception that the Vikings drank out of their enemies' skulls—a belief arising out of the mistranslation by Magnús Ólafsson of Laufás, included by Ole Worm in *Literatura runica* (1636), of the second of these lines from *Krákumál*:

> Drekkum bjór at bragði
> ór bjúgviðum hausa

> let us drink beer boldly out of curved branches of skulls [a kenning for drinking horns; the skulls are those of the animals on which the horns grew]

translated as 'ex craniis eorum quos ceciderunt' (Gordon 1957, lxix–lxx).

---

[11] Letter to James Beattie, December 1767 (Toynbee and Whibley [1935] 1971, III 983).

[12] Letter of February 1768 (Toynbee and Whibley [1935] 1971, III 1011).

[13] Letter to George Montagu, May 1761. Walpole further refers to the original plan for the incorporation of the Odes in a literary history, with a waspish but prophetic comment on Gray's dilatoriness: 'They are to be enchased in a history of English bards, which Mason and he are Writing; but of which the former has not written a word yet, and of which the latter, if he rides Pegasus at his usual footpace, will finish the first page two years hence.' (Wright [1840] 1842, III 123).

[14] Letter to George Montagu, March 1768 (Wright [1840] 1842, III 516).

Despite Gray's energetic search for highly coloured images and his popular success, the academic origin of the enterprise is still visible in the presentation of the poems. Each has a learned apparatus of footnotes, such as the accurate account of the valkyries referred to before, which is attached to line 1 of the 'The Fatal Sisters'. This includes the correct Old Norse plural form *valkyriur*, although the word itself never actually appears in the poem or in its Old Norse original. Given that there are footnotes at all, in fact, we might expect more explanation and contextualization of what is going on in the poems. The footnotes are actually rather few, and in both poems are concentrated at the beginning of the text, in order to give the appearance of learned commentary rather than the reality.

The question whether Gray had any first-hand knowledge of Scandinavian languages has been debated at some length (Lonsdale 1969, 210–14; Omberg 1976, 41–42). It seems clear that he did not, although he had read widely in the learned literature in Latin, still the *lingua franca* of scholarship in this field, some of which cited the Icelandic texts as well as translating them; and it is clear that Gray took some interest in the original language: witness the citation of the first line of each poem in the original. His notes in his Commonplace Books include the occasional addition of a word or more of the original. An example of his awareness of the original language comes in the first line of 'The Descent of Odin'. Gray's source began from the first line of stanza two of *Baldrs draumar*: 'Upp reis Óðinn', which he renders 'Up rose the King of Men . . .' reproducing the word order of the original and taking advantage of the linguistic similarity. Margaret Clunies Ross (1998, 116 n. 21) notes that in Gray's autograph versions 'uprose' appears as one word, imitating the Icelandic form which, in the version he used, was also rendered as a single word.

The use made by Gray of his Latin sources is analysed by Lonsdale (1969, 213), and Clunies Ross and Omberg comment further. A full exploration of the subject would require the presentation of Gray's texts in full, alongside the Latin texts and the Old Norse originals used by the Latin translators, and is not attempted here. The comments below are confined to some examples of how Gray's texts differ from their Old Norse originals, and the conclusions to be drawn from these about his techniques of adaptation.

'The Fatal Sisters'

Gray's Ode (Gray 1966, 27–31) follows the example of *Njáls saga* itself by contextualizing the poem with a prose preamble, locating the gruesome vision of the weaving valkyries with reference to the battle of Clontarf in 1014, in which Sigurðr, jarl of Orkney, assists the Irish king Sigtryggr silkiskegg against Brján, king of Dublin. This identification in fact sits badly with the Irish victory recorded in *Njáls saga*, since the poem refers to an apparently victorious young king (Sigtryggr?) presiding over disaster for the Irish, and it has been suggested that the poem in fact belongs to a Viking victory of 919, a date which fits better with the heathen spirit of the poem.[15] Gray's preface allows this discrepancy to pass without overt comment, rationalizing it with reference to Sigtryggr's near defeat and explaining the grief of the Irish, mentioned in the poem, with reference to the death of Brján (Gray 1966, 27):

> The Earl & all his forces were cut to pieces, & *Sictryg* was in danger of a total defeat, but the Enemy had a greater loss by the death of *Brian*, their King, who fell in the action.

For Gray, as indeed for the author of *Njáls saga*, the circumstances of the battle are of less importance than the symbolic effect of the weaving of fate, and the metaphorical contrast established between the masculine and extraordinary actions of war and the feminine and quotidian activity of weaving.

As in the saga, the vision is observed at a distance from the battle by 'a native of *Caithness*', named in the saga as Dǫrruðr—a name explained by Russell Poole as 'probably an etymological whimsy or blunder' (1991, 142) based on the difficult phrase, *vefr darraðar*, from which the poem derives its (modern) name—but anonymous in Gray's version.[16] Gray places the vision, and therefore the battle, on 'Christmas-day' rather than Good Friday, the date named in the saga; more significantly for his interpretation, the strange figures of the vision are seen riding towards, and disappearing into, not a *dyngja* 'women's work-building' with a *gluggr* 'window' but 'a hill' inside which they are observed through 'an opening in the rocks'. They are 'gigantic figures resembling Women' rather than the *konur* 'women' of the saga. Here we see Gray beginning

---

[15] This was first suggested by Nora Kershaw; see Poole 1991, 120–25.

[16] Gray's modern editors refer approvingly (Gray 1966, 211) to his avoidance of Torfaeus's erroneous rendering of *darraðar* as a proper name, translating *vefr darraðar* as *Telam Darradi* (though Torfaeus did, of course, have the authority of the *Njáls saga* prose):

> It should be noted that Gray was not misled by these renderings, having written 'web of war' both times. Indeed it seems to the present editors, whose knowledge of ON is also rather limited, that Gray did much better than he has usually been given credit for in avoiding the pitfalls of this poem.

to magnify the horrifying imagery of the poem, as he does repeatedly throughout both Odes (and, in the locating of the vision within the hill, perhaps conflating the Norse with the Celtic mythological landscape). On the other hand, his preface does not follow the saga prose where it details the horrific details of the weaving process (*Njáls saga* 454–59):

> Mannahǫfuð váru fyrir kljána, en þarma ór mǫnnum fyrir viptu ok garn, sverð var fyrir skeið, en ǫr fyrir hræl.
>
> men's heads served as loomweights and intestines from men as weft and warp, a sword as the sword-beater and an arrow as the pin-beater.[17]

This is in line with the saga convention in which verses are offered as corroboration of material presented less dramatically in prose, but Gray more artfully reserves these details for his poetic text.

Apart from a reference to 'the loom of hell', Gray's opening stanza does not derive from his source but consists of an atmospheric prelude establishing the metaphorical parallel between battle and storm:

> Now the storm begins to lower,
> (Haste, the loom of hell prepare)
> Iron-sleet of arrowy shower
> Hurtles in the darken'd air.

This metaphorical equivalence is a commonplace of skaldic poetry, as Gray presumably knew from his wider reading of Norse sources in translation, but is not referred to in *Darraðarljóð* except in the terse *rignir blóði* 'blood rains down' (l. 4). Gray explicitly associates these lines not with the Norse poetic tradition, but with the English, in footnotes highlighting his own echoing of Milton (Gray 1966, 215):

> How quick they wheel'd & flying behind them shot
> Sharp sleet of arrowy shower[s]—
>   Milton Par[adise]: Reg[ained]. [iii. 323–4]

and Shakespeare:

> The noise of battle hurtled in the air. Shakesp: Jul: Caesar [II. ii. 22].

This transformation perfectly illustrates Gray's use of his Odes as a general introduction to the 'spirit' of northern literature rather than a faithful representation of his originals, and also his ambitions of transforming this spirit into an idiom recognizable from—and by implication, related to—the English poetic canon. It also, in fact, demonstrates the con-

---

[17] I cite the translation of Russell Poole (1991, 119), who analyses the technological terms used in the poem in detail. As he points out, it 'constitut[es] our only detailed medieval account' of the process (132–33).

straints imposed by the scholarly limitations of his time, for the imagery of the cloud of arrows is clearly inspired by the misunderstood kenning *rifs reiðiský*. This phrase, translated by Russell Poole as 'the hanging cloud of the loom beam' (1991, 132)[18] refers to the 'cloth' produced by the weaving process, but was misunderstood by the Latin translator who renders it *nubes sagittarum* 'cloud of arrows'. A similar misunderstanding of Old Norse metaphor occurs at the end of Gray's third stanza, where the valkyries' self-identifying reference to themselves as *vinur Randvés bana* 'female friends of the slayer of Randvér' (i.e. of Óðinn who, according to Old Norse heroic legend, brought about the killing of Randvér, son of Jǫrmunrekkr) was inaccessible to both Latin and English translators. Gray chooses to imply that the name refers to an otherwise unmentioned victim of the fate determined by the valkyries, in a neatly constructed parallel with the downfall of the Orkney jarl, alluded to in the prose preamble:

> Weaving many a Soldier's doom,
> *Orkney*'s woe, and *Randver*'s bane.

Gray adapts the poem's form to the conventions of his time. The eleven stanzas of *Darraðarljóð*, of variable length (8–10 lines, apart from the final quatrain) are rendered by Gray's sixteen stanzas, in the regular metre and rhyme scheme of the so-called 'Horatian Ode'. The only concession to the form of the original is the rendering of the thrice-repeated refrain *Vindum vindum / vef darraðar* with '(Weave the crimson web of war.)', which occurs twice in Gray's version, though not at the same points as in the original.

Gray's regular intensification of the gruesome imagery of his original is illustrated by his version of the second stanza. The Icelandic text is cited here with Russell Poole's translation (1991, 116) alongside:

sá er orpinn vefr	The fabric is warped
ýta þǫrmum	with men's intestines
ok harðkljáðr	and firmly weighted
hǫfðum manna;	with men's heads;
eru dreyrrekin	bloodstained spears serve
dǫrr at skǫptum,	as heddle rods,
járnvarðr yllir	the shed rod is ironclad
en ǫrum ?hælaðr?.	and ?pegged? with arrows.
Skulum slá sverðum	With our swords we must strike
sigrvef þenna.	this fabric of victory.

The technical details of the weaving craft, inaccessible to the modern reader, would presumably have been less so in Gray's day, but rather

---

[18] For detailed analysis of the kenning see Clunies Ross 1998, 114.

than pursuing the minutiae of the metaphor, Gray heightens the language, mainly with the addition of intensifying adjectives ('griesly', 'gasping', 'trembling'):

> See the griesly texture grow,
> ('Tis of human entrails made)
> And the weights, that play below
> Each a gasping Warriour's head.
>
> Shafts for shuttles, dipt in gore,
> Shoot the trembling cords along.
> Sword, that once a Monarch bore,
> Keep the tissue close & strong!

Gray's choice of names for his valkyries is enterprising; he understands that the names given to these entities are representative, variable according to metrical requirements, and is able to draw on his own learned researches for substitutes that fit his own purposes, so the *Hildr* [. . .] *ok Hǫrþrimul, Sanngríðr, Svipul* and later *Gunnr ok Gǫndul* of his original are represented in

> *Mista* black, terrific Maid,
> *Sangrida*, and *Hilda* see
> [. . .]:
> *Gondula* and *Geira*, spread
> O'er the youthful King your shield.

The actual function of the valkyries—whether their weaving signifies their actual determination, by a process conceived of as magic, of the outcome of the distant battle or merely an omen or a visual representation of its events—is left obscure by the original poem (the point is discussed by Poole (1991, 140–41)). The very last line of Gray's rendition, 'Hurry, hurry to the field', suggests that this question was resolved in his mind by an assumption that the valkyries are progressing from the prefiguring of the battle in the vision to actual participation in the slaughter, where *Darraðarljóð* itself simply has the speakers riding out *á braut heðan* 'away from here'.

'The Descent of Odin'

The somewhat less regular form of Gray's second Ode (Gray 1966, 32–34) is partly determined by the casting of its original, *Baldrs draumar*, like many eddic poems, in dialogue form: in this case, Óðinn's interrogation of a *vǫlva*, forcibly raised from the dead, about the fate in store for his doomed son, Baldr. In this poem, as in Gray's version, the dialogue exchange determines the structure; but whereas the division of *Baldrs draumar* into eight-line stanzas is comparatively regular by eddic standards, Gray divides his poem into blocks, varying in length, of rhyming couplets. The epic effect aimed for is intensified by his free expansion of the original, concentrating on effects he sees as particularly grotesque or picturesque. For instance, Óðinn's encounter with the canine guardian of the underworld is sparely narrated in the original:[19]

mœtti hann hvelpi,	he met a hound-whelp
þeim er ór Heliu kom.	that came out of Hel.
Sá var blóðugr	It was bloody
um brióst framan,	down the front of its breast,
ok galdrs fǫður	and round wizardry's father
gó *um* lengi.	went barking long.

This is considerably elaborated by Gray, clearly with the aim of injecting a note of terror, and with characteristic use of favourite terms such as 'gore' and 'carnage':

> Him the Dog of darkness spied:
> His shaggy throat he open'd wide,
> While from his jaws, with carnage fill'd
> Foam & human gore distill'd:
> Hoarse he bays with hideous din,
> Eyes, that glow, and fangs that grin,
> And long pursues with fruitless yell
> The Father of the powerful spell.

Probably also behind Gray's selection of this image for expansion is his eagerness to find parallels (in this case the hound Cerberus) in the classical mythology so familiar to himself and his audience; this also underlies his footnote explicating the Norse belief in the underworld. In the poem this is described as 'Hela's drear abode' (rendering *Heljar ranni* 'the hall of Hel' in *Baldrs draumar* 3), with the footnote

> *Niflheimr*, the hell of the Gothic nations, consisted of nine worlds,[20] to which were devoted all such as died of sickness, old-age, or by any other means than in battle: Over it presided Hela, the Goddess of Death.

---

[19] Text and translation are quoted from the edition of Ursula Dronke (1997, 154).

[20] Starr and Hendrickson note that this reference, and the specifying of 'nine portals' in the poem, seem to derive from the statement in *Gylfaginning* (Snorri Sturluson 1982, 27) that Óðinn cast Hel *í Niflheim ok gaf henni vald yfir níu heimum* 'into Niflheimr and gave her power over nine worlds', although the nine worlds referred to must be the nine regions making up the cosmos (see *Vǫluspá* 2 (Dronke 1997, 7) and Anthony Faulkes's note in Snorri Sturluson 1982, 65) rather than nine regions of Niflheimr as in Gray's interpretation. It is not known what access Gray had to Snorri's reference (Gray 1966, 219).

This degree of detail, which is gratuitous from the point of view of comprehension of the poem, demonstrates Gray's interest in Germanic mythology for its own sake and his desire to share it with his contemporaries. He also inserts into the poem itself a specificity beyond that of the original in referring to 'the portals nine of hell' and locating Óðinn's encounter 'right against the eastern gate' (*fyrr austan dyrr* 'to the east of the door' in *Baldrs draumar*). Gray's mythological preoccupations are rather specific, however: he is particularly interested in the conceptualizing of the underworld and the surrounding imagery of death and doom. Óðinn is accorded little interest and the colourless epithet 'King of Men' for the *alda gautr, aldinn gautr* of the original,[21] and the Æsir are the 'sons of heaven' without further distinction. *Baldrs draumar* implies that Óðinn's son Váli was conceived in order to achieve vengeance for Baldr, and says outright that he did so at the age of one night; Gray passes over the drama of this story.

A different kind of expansion is seen in Gray's elaborate image for the mead which, the *vǫlva* (or Prophetess, in Gray's version) tells Óðinn, awaits Baldr in the underworld:

> *Pr.* Mantling in the goblet see
> The pure bev'rage of the bee,
> O'er it hangs the shield of gold;
> 'Tis the drink of *Balder* bold.

The periphrastic elaboration of *mjǫðr* 'mead' as 'the pure beverage of the bee' represents a characteristic poetic habit of the poet who refers elsewhere to the play of schoolboys who

> succeed
> To chase the rolling circle's speed
> Or urge the flying ball[22]

---

[21] This may be explained by the 'motto' Gray appended to the poem: '*gautr* is of uncertain meaning' (Gray 1966, 218). This is still only too true. *Gautr* is found elsewhere as a name for Óðinn, and is usually identified with the tribal names for the Goths and *Gautar*. But other explanations have been attempted: thus, 'it seems to mean *father*, vide gjóta [to spawn]' (Cleasby and Vigfusson 1874, *s.v.* 'gautar'), and 'one intended or consecrated as a sacrificial victim' (La Farge and Tucker 1992, 81), followed in Dronke's translation, 'aged god of sacrifice' (1997, 154, 156). The latter interpretation appears to be pure conjecture, based on the context in *Baldrs draumar*. I am grateful for advice on this point to Anthony Faulkes, who suggests 'progenitor of the human race' for *alda gautr* (based on the probable relationship of *gautr* with *gjóta*).

[22] 'Ode on a Distant Prospect of Eton College' (Gray 1966, 8). On the artifice of Gray's diction, see Spacks 1965.

a generalizing tendency comparable to the metaphorical habits of mind of the skaldic poets, though its technique is different. It is classical in origins and, in this case, probably represents Gray's attempts to align this poem with the epic tradition.

Baldrs draumar concludes, like other dialogue poems involving Óðinn, with a riddling question that exposes the identity of the god; he in turn identifies the *vǫlva* as *þriggja þursa móðir* 'mother of three monsters'. The details are elusive; it is not clear why the god's question is put or indeed what the answer should be (it is usually taken to refer to the waves), nor how it reveals his identity—except, perhaps, by the general situational similarity with poems like *Vafþrúðnismál*, where the mysterious inquirer into similar matters does turn out to be Óðinn. Gray offers no speculation on these questions, nor on the identification, which the mythologically informed Norse audience was no doubt intended to make, of the *vǫlva* with Angrboða, the mother of Loki's three monstrous children.

The giantess's final taunt predicts the destruction of the world and the gods at Ragnarǫk, and relies on allusiveness for its effect. The reference to Loki has been prepared for by Óðinn's implied identification of her; and the naming of *ragnarǫk* of course conjures up, to those versed in its mythological implications, the disaster that makes ironic the injunction to Óðinn to *ver hróðigr* 'rejoice':

Heim ríð þú, Óðinn,	Ride home, Óðinn,
ok ver hróðigr!	and exult!
Svá komit manna	No one will come
meirr aptr á vit,	back again on such a visit,
er lauss Loki	when Loki, freed,
líðr ór bǫndum	moves from his bonds
ok ragnarǫk	and Ragnarǫk
riúfendr koma.	arrives with ruin.

Gray's paraphrase both provides his readers with some necessary exposition, and ends the poem in a melodramatic blaze:

> *Pr.* Hie thee hence & boast at home,
> That never shall Enquirer come
> To break my iron-sleep again:
> Till *Lok* has burst his tenfold chain,
> Never, till substantial Night
> Has reassum'd her ancient right;
> Till wrap'd in flames, in ruin hurl'd,
> Sinks the fabrick of the world.

The final footnote, though, reaffirms the scholarly impulse that underlay Gray's quest for the sensational (Gray 1966, 220):

Lok is the evil Being, who continues in chains till the *Twilight of the Gods* approaches, when he shall break his bonds; the human race, the stars, & sun, shall disappear; the earth sink in the seas, & fire consume the skies; even Odin himself and his kindred-Deities shall perish. For a farther explanation of this mythology, see Mallet's Introduction to the History of Denmark, 1755, Quarto.

Thus Gray lays the climactic moment of Old Norse mythology before his readers in two contrasting modes: one, the dramatic visionary effects of poetry, the other, the authority of the learned note, complete with reference to an authoritative source. The dualism fittingly illustrates the two impulses behind his approach to his mythological sources.

Bibliography

Austen, Jane 1933. *The Novels of Jane Austen. The Text Based on Collation of the Early Editions*. Ed. R. W. Chapman. 5 vols. 3rd edition. V: *Northanger Abbey* and *Persuasion*.

Bartholin, Thomas 1689. *Antiquitatum Danicarum de causis contemptæ a Danis adhuc gentilibus mortis*.

Burke, Edmund 1757. *A Philosophical Enquiry into the Origin of our Ideas of the Sublime and Beautiful*.

Cleasby, R. and Gudbrand Vigfusson 1874. *An Icelandic-English Dictionary*.

Clunies Ross, Margaret 1998. *The Norse Muse in Britain 1750–1820*.

Coleridge, Samuel Taylor and William Wordsworth 1802. *Lyrical Ballads* I.

Dronke, Ursula, ed. and trans., 1997. *The Poetic Edda* II: *Mythological Poems*.

Gordon, E. V. 1957. *An Introduction to Old Norse*. 2nd edn, revised A. R. Taylor.

Gray, Thomas. *Commonplace Books* I–III (Unpublished), Pembroke College, Cambridge.

Gray, Thomas 1966. *The Complete Poems of Thomas Gray. English, Latin, and Greek*. Ed. H. W. Starr and J. R. Hendrickson.

Hickes, George 1705. *Linguarum vett. septentrionalium thesaurus grammatico-criticus et archæologicus*.

La Farge, Beatrice and John Tucker, eds, 1992. *Glossary to the Poetic Edda: Based on Hans Kuhn's Kurzes Wörterbuch*.

Lonsdale, Roger, ed., 1969. *The Poems of Thomas Gray, William Collins, Oliver Goldsmith*.

Macpherson, James 1762. *Fingal, an Ancient Epic Poem in Six Books: Together with Several Other Books, Composed by Ossian the Son of Fingal. Translated from the Galic Language, by James Macpherson*.

Macpherson, James 1763. *Temora, an Ancient Epic Poem in Eight Books: Together with Several Other Poems Composed by Ossian, the Son of Fingal. Translated from the Galic Language, by James Macpherson*.

Mallet, Paul Henri 1755. *Introduction à l'histoire de Dannemarc, où l'on traite de la religion, des loix, des moeurs et des usages des anciens Danois*.

Már Jónsson 1998. *Árni Magnússon. Ævisaga.*
Njáls saga=Einar Ol. Sveinsson, ed., 1954. *Brennu-Njáls saga*. Íslenzk fornrit XII.
Omberg, Margaret 1976. *Scandinavian Themes in English Poetry, 1760–1800.*
Poole, Russell 1991. *Viking Poems on War and Peace.*
Snorri Sturluson 1941–51. *Heimskringla.* Ed. Bjarni Aðalbjarnarson. Íslenzk fornrit XXVI–XXVIII.
Snorri Sturluson 1982. *Edda. Prologue and Gylfaginning.* Ed. Anthony Faulkes.
Spacks, Patricia Meyer 1965. 'Statement and Artifice in Thomas Gray'. *Studies in English Literature, 1500–1900* 5:3, 519–32.
Stokes, Francis Griffin, ed., 1929. *An Elegy Written in a Country Church Yard by Thomas Gray; The Text of the First Quarto with the Variants of the mss. & of the Early Editions (1751–71), a Bibliographical & Historical Introduction & Appendices on General Wolfe & The 'Elegy' & The Locality of the Churchyard by Francis Griffin Stokes.*
Temple, William 1690. *Miscellanea. The Second Part. In Four Essays.*
Torfæus, Thormod [Þormóðr Torfason] 1697. *Orcades, seu rerum Orcadensium historiæ libri tres.*
Toynbee, Paget and Leonard Whibley, eds, [1935] 1971. *The Correspondence of Thomas Gray.* 3 vols.
Warton, Thomas 1774. *The History of English Poetry* I.
Worm, Ole 1636. *Runir seu Danica literatura antiquissima.*
Wright, J., ed., [1840] 1842. *The Letters of Horace Walpole, Earl of Orford. Including Numerous Letters Now First Published from the Original Manuscripts.* 4 vols.

The Thomas Gray archive: http://www.thomasgray.org/index.shtml

TRANSLATING THE *POETIC EDDA* INTO ENGLISH[1]

CAROLYNE LARRINGTON

Early Knowledge of Norse Mythology

Norse mythology, and the poetry and prose which recounted or alluded to it, was known about in England from the seventeenth century (see Quinn and Clunies Ross 1994 for a summary and the unpublished thesis of Bennett 1938 for detail). The Codex Regius, containing the great majority of the poems that we now classify as eddic, was sent to Copenhagen from Iceland by Bishop Brynjólfur Sveinsson in 1643, and was subsequently catalogued as GKS 2365 4to. In 1665 Peder Hans Resen published an edition of *Vǫluspá* and *Hávamál*, providing them with a Latin translation, though he did not make use of the Codex Regius as a basis for his texts (so Clunies Ross 1998, 180; *contra* Wawn 2000, 18 who suggests that Resen did employ the Codex Regius). With the addition of a text of Snorri's *Edda*, the Resen volume introduced Norse mythological poetry to the world (Quinn and Clunies Ross 1994, 193). The first reference to this work in England is in the Preface to Robert Sheringham's *De Anglorum gentis origine disceptatio*, published in 1670 (see Quinn and Clunies Ross 1994, 193 n. 12). Moreover, a copy of Resen's *Edda* was given to the Bodleian Library in Oxford in the early 1670s. Aylett Sammes seems to have been the first to translate part of an eddic poem (the Loddfáfnir stanzas of *Hávamál*) into English (Sammes 1676, 442ff), though his source was Sheringham's citation of these verses in Latin, rather than Resen's Old Norse text.

The Swiss antiquarian Paul Henri Mallet wrote a two-volume account of early Scandinavian beliefs and history in 1755 and 1766, entitled *Introduction à l'histoire de Dannemarc* and *Monumens de la mythologie et de la poésie des Celtes*. Like many of his contemporaries, Mallet believed that the Northern races were Celtic in origin, hence his title. In his work Mallet summarized parts of *Vǫluspá*, quoted from *Hávamál* in

---

[1] This essay originates in a talk given to the Viking Society Student Conference in 1997, before the publication of some substantial works on the reception of the *Poetic Edda* in England in the eighteenth and nineteenth centuries. It has been extensively revised to take account of Clunies Ross 1998 and Wawn 2000.

French translation, and also reproduced the first few verses of *Baldrs draumar* which had been published by the Danish scholar Thomas Bartholin (Bartholin 1689). Mallet's Introduction was translated into English by Bishop Thomas Percy under the title *Northern Antiquities* in 1770. Thus it was primarily from Mallet and then from Percy that English Romantic writers learned about Norse myth and heroic legend. They made 'versions' of the Norse heroic poems they found in the earlier works. Most notable was Thomas Gray's 'The Descent of Odin', expanding upon Mallet's excerpts from *Baldrs draumar* and the verses in Bartholin (see Finlay in this volume). Gray published this and his other Norse Ode in 1768 (Clunies Ross 1998, 105–09). Percy himself offered 'Five Pieces of Runick Poetry' (Clunies Ross 2001) which were published in 1763. Although he was aware of the Resen versions of the first two poems of the Codex Regius, Percy did not include any of the texts normally considered part of the *Poetic Edda* in his collection. In 1787 the Arnamagnæan Commission in Copenhagen began to publish a fully edited text of the Codex Regius and other eddic poems, at last permitting proper scholarly study and translation of the contents. The Copenhagen *Edda* reserved re-editing *Vǫluspá* and *Hávamál* to the third volume, on the grounds that Resen had already provided texts of them (however inadequate in terms both of textual soundness and of scholarly apparatus). Volume I of the Copenhagen *Poetic Edda* not only furnished texts of the rest of the mythological poetry of the Codex Regius, but also provided a useful Latin apparatus. This, as Clunies Ross puts it, was 'user-friendly for scholars who were neither native speakers of Icelandic nor trained in Old Norse studies' (1998, 180–81). The possibility of translating eddic verse into English from an Old Norse original, with the help of a Latin translation and the substantial Copenhagen glossary, now existed. This essay considers the translations of Cottle (1797), Herbert (1804, 1806, and 1842), Thorpe (1866), Vigfusson and York Powell (1883), Bray (1908), Bellows (1926), Hollander (1928), Terry (1969), Auden, Taylor, and Salus (1969) as well as Larrington (1996), the expanded Auden and Taylor (1981), and Dronke (1969, 1997).

What is the Poetic Edda?

Translators are faced with choices about what to include in their versions of the *Poetic Edda* even before they begin to think about larger translation principles. For early translators such decisions were limited by the availability of edited texts. Although neither of the terms 'eddic' and 'eddaic' was used in English until the middle of the nineteenth century, 'Edda' is first used in James Macpherson's *An Introduction to the History of Great Britain and Ireland* (1771, 180) referring most likely to Resen's edition. Although the core of eddic verse is the collection of poems from *Vǫluspá* to *Hamðismál* contained in GKS 2365 4to, other poems in eddic metre such as *Hrafnagaldur Óðins*, *Sólarljóð* or *Svipdagsmál* have been included in editions and translations at various times, along with the now more-or-less canonical *Baldrs draumar*, *Grottasǫngr*, *Rígsþula* and *Hyndloljóð*. Many *fornaldarsögur* contain verses in eddic metre (edited in Ranisch and Heusler, 1903). 'The Waking of Angantýr', the 'Riddles of Gestumblindi', and 'The Battle of the Goths and Huns', all contained in *Hervarar saga ok Heiðreks*, are often candidates for inclusion in eddic translations. The obscure *Hrafnagaldur Óðins* appears in Thorpe's translation of 1866, but is generally excluded from the canon thereafter, although Annette Lassen (2006) has recently argued that it may indeed be a genuine (late-) medieval poem. Hollander asserts that *Svipdagsmál* is 'undoubtedly genuine', though this view would by no means command universal agreement (Hollander 1936, xv). No later translators include it in their canon.

Early Translations: Cottle and Herbert

Problems of contextualization, the publisher's and reader's tolerance of extensive apparatus and questions of contemporary taste have always affected the choices *Edda* translators make. Clunies Ross points out the practical difficulties facing early translators, who lacked Icelandic dictionaries and for whom the understanding of the complex mythology underlying such an allusive poem as *Vǫluspá* was nigh impossible to obtain. Furthermore, since eighteenth-century literary theorists, and their nineteenth-century followers, had 'strongly-held ideas about what ancient poetry was like' this led them 'to seek out poems that they thought exemplified their ideas, and thus to prefer a free over an exact translation' (Clunies Ross 1998, 25). Such freedom of style and interpretation is marked in Gray's 'The Descent of Odin', and in the work of the earliest translator of entire eddic poems: Amos Cottle. Cottle's *Icelandic Poetry, or the Edda of Sæmund* was published in Bristol in 1797, and, as Wawn notes (2000, 195–96), was based on the Latin translations in the first volume of the Copenhagen *Edda*, available in the Bristol Public Library and borrowed by such notables as Robert Southey (Pratt 1994 gives a full account of the Bristol coterie).

Following the first volume of the Copenhagen *Edda*, Cottle thus includes the mythological poetry from *Vafþrúðnismál* to *Alvíssmál*, plus

Hrafnagaldur Óðins, *Vegtamskviða* (an earlier name for *Baldrs draumar*), *Fjölsvinnsmál*, and *Hyndloljóð*. *Vǫluspá* and *Hávamál* are omitted, as they were from the first volume of the Copenhagen *Edda*. Cottle attaches a substantial and learned introduction to his translations; since he rightly assumes that his readership will be most familiar with Greek mythology he develops a lengthy comparison between the Norse deities and the Greek pantheon. Based on rather superficial resemblances, this results in some surprising assertions for the modern scholar of Norse myth. Thus Odin 'appears to be the Northern Adonis. He was beloved by Frigga, who represents Venus, and is killed at last by a Wolf, as Adonis was by a boar' (Cottle 1797, xxiii). Likewise, 'Lok may be compared to the Apollo of the Grecians' (Cottle 1797, xxiii). Cottle provides very little discussion of his translation methods, doubtless because of his ignorance of Old Norse. This leads him into considerable error, most notably in *Þrymskviða* (see below), but elsewhere too, where he proves incapable even of translating the Latin accurately. William Herbert, who could read Icelandic, knew Danish, and who offered the first part of his *Select Icelandic Poetry* to the public in 1804, criticizes the hapless Cottle without reservation: 'Mr Cottle has published, what he calls a translation of this ode, but it bears little resemblance to the original. [...] Mr C. has not even taken the trouble of understanding the Latin' (Herbert 1842, I, 179; see also 180 and 193). Cottle's *Edda*, like Herbert's, does not seem to have been widely circulated. In the preface to the first volume of *The Edda of Sæmund the Learned* (1866, I) Benjamin Thorpe notes 'this work [Cottle's] I have never met with; nor have I seen any English version of any part of the Edda, with the exception of Gray's spirited but free translation of the Vegtamskviða' (Thorpe 1866, vii). Notwithstanding Herbert's justifiable criticism of his predecessor's accuracy, Cottle often achieves a romantic grandeur in his versions of the poems.

Herbert's own versions of eddic poetry were published piecemeal. Of what is now considered to be the *Poetic Edda* corpus, Volume I of *Select Icelandic Poetry* (1804) contained only *Þrymskviða* and a few verses of *Baldrs draumar*. The second volume of 1806 added *Helreið Brynhildar* and *Skirnismál* to the tally. In 1839 he translated *Sigurðarkviða in skamma* and *Atlakviða* from volume II of the Copenhagen *Edda* (see Clunies Ross 1998, 188). *Vǫlundarkviða* followed in 1840; all three new poems were included in *Horae Scandicae: Or, Works Relating to Old Scandinavian Literature*, the first volume of Herbert's complete works, published in 1842. Clunies Ross (1998, 183–202) gives a detailed account of Herbert's sources and assesses his relative success in translating

Þrymskviða and *Helreið* in *Select Icelandic Poetry*. Herbert represents his translations as 'closely translated and unadorned; with a few exceptions they are rendered line for line; and (I believe) as literally, as the difference of language and metrical rules would permit' (Herbert 1842, 167), modestly averring, 'the only merit I have aimed at, is that of accuracy' (1804, ix). As Clunies Ross shows (1998, 183–84), he amply persuades his reviewers of his mastery of Icelandic language, even though he often goes considerably beyond his source text, mostly in pursuit of a rhyme. Herbert contrasts 'the energetic harmony of these old poems: [. . .] the most ancient are the simplest and most beautiful', with skaldic verse, which he, like a number of other translators, understands as younger than the *Edda*, 'for the Icelandic poetry degenerated into affectation of impenetrable obscurity and extravagant metaphors' (Herbert 1842, 167). Herbert also composed poems based very loosely on Norse myth, such as *Hedin* (from the Hjaðningavíg myth) and, from the *Poetic Edda*, *The Song of Vala*, which was 'freely imitated from a curious old poem called Völospá hin skamre [sic], or the ancient Prophecy of Vala, which forms part of the unpublished Edda' (Herbert 1842, 147).

Victorian versions

The noted Anglo-Saxon scholar Benjamin Thorpe somewhat diffidently issued the first volume of his translation of the *Poetic Edda* in 1866, promising that 'if a not unfavourable reception is given it by the British public, the Second, or Heroic part shall be immediately sent to press' (Thorpe 1866, I viii). *The Edda of Sæmund the Learned* was based on a German edition (Lüning 1859; see Wawn 2000, 196–97) and includes the mythological poems of the Codex Regius, plus *Fjölsvinnsmál*, *Rígsþula*, *Hyndloljóð*, *Gróugaldr*, and *Sólarljóð* (a text which Cottle had rejected on the grounds that it was 'filled with little else but the absurd superstitions of the Church of Rome' (1797, xxix–xxx)). Thorpe's work is largely accurate and pleasingly simple; the translator modestly claims, 'it had no pretension to elegance; but I believe it to be a faithful though homely representation of the original' (Thorpe 1866, I viii). Volume II did indeed follow later in the same year, after positive reviews: 'For not only has its reception been favourable, but in the United States of America it has been noticed in terms highly gratifying to the translator' (1866, II iii). To the Codex Regius heroic poems, Thorpe added *Grottasǫngr* and 'Gunnars Slagr' (1866, II 146–49), a poem preserved only in paper manuscripts and translated from Rask's edition published in Stockholm (Rask 1818). Thorpe's translations, often surprisingly modern in tone, tend to eschew archaism and Latinisms. Wawn (2000, 196) suggests that Thorpe appears to take some liberties in re-ordering the Icelandic text when he translates some verses from *Vǫluspá* (Neckel and Kuhn 1962, vv. 45–46), an effect produced by the translator's faithful rendition of Lüning's text. The German editor collates lines from the Hauksbók and Codex Uppsaliensis manuscripts of *Vǫluspá* with the Codex Regius text, producing a Norse version that looks unfamiliar to those used to the Copenhagen *Edda* (Thorpe 1866, I 9; Lüning 1859, 150–51).

No other substantial translations of the *Edda* appeared in the nineteenth century except for Vigfusson and York Powell's work in *Corpus Poeticum Boreale* (1883), though the notable Icelandic scholar Eiríkr Magnússon had his translation rejected (Wawn 2000, 195, n. 65) and that of his compatriot Jón Hjaltalín was never published (Wawn 2000, 362). Eiríkr Magnússon and William Morris did, however, offer some versions of those heroic poems relevant to *Vǫlsunga saga* in their 1870 translation of that work, *The Story of the Volsungs and Niblungs, with certain songs from the Elder Edda*; these are the last part of *Helgakviða Hundingsbana II*, the wisdom section of *Sigrdrífumál*, *Sigurðarkviða in skamma*, *Helreið Brynhildar*, *Brot* (rechristened *Fragments of the Lay of Brynhild*), *Guðrúnarkviða II*, *Atlakviða*, *Guðrúnarhvǫt*, and *Hamðismál*, with the addition of *Oddrúnargrátr*, 'which we have translated on account of its intrinsic merit', the authors note (Magnússon and Morris 1870, x). The authors make a close comparison between the eddic poems and the content of the saga, noting of the episode of Sigrún and Helgi in the burial mound: 'for the the sake of its wonderful beauty however, we could not refrain from rendering it' (vii). The authors are aware that the material may offer some difficulty, but exhort the reader to effort:

> we may well trust the reader of poetic insight to break through whatever entanglement of strange manners, [. . .] such a reader will be intensely touched by finding, amidst all its wildness and remoteness, such startling realism, such subtilty, such close sympathy with all the passions that may move himself today (x–xi).

Vigfusson and York Powell divide up the poems of the Codex Regius according to their presumed chronology, their hypothetical place of origin, and their supposed author, such as 'the Western Aristophanes', author of *Lokasenna*, *Hárbarðzljóð*, and *Skírnismál*. Vigfusson and York Powell discuss the principles of their prose translations, which run along the bottom of the page of their edition, in the introduction to volume I (cxiv–xvii). They maintain that the translation has no pretension to literary merit, but is merely a guide to assist those who wish to read the poems 'without having mastered the tongues in which they are composed' (cxiv). The enterprise is not simple, despite its limited goals: for the translator must render the different styles of the poets: 'the legal phrases of the Greenland Lay of Attila and the Euripidean softness of the Gudrun lays are very far removed from the antique Homeric beauty of the old Attila and Hamtheow Lays' (cxv), they note; like Cottle and Herbert before them they employ familiar parallels from classical literature to characterize the Norse. The sternest observations are reserved for the mere philologist who becomes 'a gerund-grinding machine' (cxv), who fails to immerse himself in a detailed study of the 'old life' (cxiv) and thus misses the literary qualities of the poems. Particularly castigated are those translators of Norse who fall into 'the affectation of archaism, and the abuse of archaic Scottish, pseudo-Middle English words' (cxv), a criticism no doubt meant for such enthusiasts as Eiríkr Magnússon and William Morris. Though Vigfusson and York Powell have opted for 'the real meaning' rather than 'the poetical rendering' they omit obscure and obscene phrases, so as not to mislead or offend the reader. Noteworthy, too, in this preface is the appeal to 'Englishmen and Americans to seek back for themselves into the Homeric age of their forefathers' (cxvii); like Thorpe, the two Oxford scholars are well aware of the importance of the American market.

Twentieth-Century Translations

The early twentieth century brought a small flurry of eddic translations, with the first American versions appearing in the 1920s. Olive Bray's *The Elder or Poetic Edda* appeared in 1908, under the auspices of the Viking Club (later to become the Viking Society). Bray was very conscious of the vivid visual images which the mythological poems produced, and attributes some translation difficulties to their interference:

> For their style is so essentially graphic without being descriptive that the more familiar we are with their works, the more difficult does it seem to translate them into words instead of colour and form (Bray 1908, i).

No wonder then that the edition is freely illustrated with striking black-and-white drawings by W. G. Collingwood. Bray edits and translates only the mythological poetry of the Codex Regius, plus the two *Svipdagsmál* poems; her introduction captures the romantic aura which the Old North held for enthusiasts of the Viking Club, at the same time as it apologizes for its un-Greek qualities:

> For mythology is itself a tangled garden of thought unless it has undergone complete transformation in the hands of the artist. It is nothing less than the mind of the nation laid bare [. . .] all stamped by past experience, but never blended into unity (vi).

Her translation aspires to literalness:

> to satisfy truth and for fear of doing injustice to the original, we have endeavoured to keep the translation as literal as possible, though ambiguity in the original occasionally necessitates interpretation by a somewhat freer rendering (i).

Quinn (1994, 120–22) discusses Bray's edition in the context of the activities and inquiring spirit of the Viking Club in the early years of the twentieth century.

Bellows selected the poems of the Codex Regius, plus *Baldrs draumar*, *Hyndloljóð*, and *Svipdagsmál*, for his translation, noting Thorpe's translation as 'conspicuously inadequate', Vigfusson and York Powell's as 'unsatisfactory', but praising Bray's work as 'excellent' (Bellows 1926, xi). Published by the American-Scandinavian Foundation in 1923, Bellows's was the first American translation, offered with the hope that

> greater familiarity with the chief literary monuments of the North will help Americans to a better understanding of Scandinavians and thus serve to stimulate their sympathetic coöperation to good ends (Bellows 1926, facing title page epigraph).

Bellows aimed to help scholars, and to stimulate others to learn the language, but, in keeping with the aims of the Foundation, he 'place[s] the hope that this English version may give to some, who have known little of the ancient traditions of what is after all their own race, a clearer insight into the glories of that extraordinary past'. Bellows implies a readership not simply of first- or second-generation immigrants from Scandinavia to North America, but makes a larger assumption that the 'glories' are the heritage of Anglo-Saxon and German Americans alike. Cord's foreword to a 1991 reprint praises the work in terms which have not normally been employed since World War II:

> the translator has overcome formidable linguistic barriers as well as certain cultural implications to convert the original Icelandic (Old Norse) poems into verse forms in English that retain, and even project, the essence of the original Teutonic ambience (Bellows 1991, i).

'Teutonic ambience', produced largely by archaic diction, is precisely what most postwar translators try to avoid—once, as Quinn notes, 'the sinister potential of Aryan ideologising had become evident' (1994, 124).

Hollander's translation is still frequently reprinted, the eleventh printing of the second revised edition appearing as recently as 2004. The selection is relatively conservative, consisting of the Codex Regius poems, *Hyndloljóð*, with *Vǫluspá in skamma* printed separately, *Rígsþula*, *Grottasǫngr*, and *Baldrs draumar*. *Svipdagsmál* is included, and the *Dvergatal* of *Vǫluspá* is also dealt with separately (Hollander 1936). Hollander notes that 'still other lays of Eddic quality' exist, translated in an earlier volume (Hollander 1962, xv, n.). He is thoughtful about the problems of reflecting the broad range of synonyms available in Norse and finds that these can only be reproduced in English through recourse to archaic equivalents, despite Vigfusson and York Powell's comments on this practice (see above): 'I have, therefore, unhesitatingly had recourse, whenever necessary, to terms fairly common in English balladry, without, I hope overloading the page with archaisms' (Hollander 1962, xxix).

Auden and Taylor's influential selection of poems was published in London in 1969, the same year that Patricia Terry's *Poems of the Vikings* appeared in Indianapolis. The introduction to the first of these, written by Peter Salus and Paul Taylor, explains metre and quantity and the details of Norse cosmology, with a particular excursus on riddles and charms. No reflection on translation practice, beyond questions of rhythm and caesura, is offered, however, except for a warning of silent rearrangement of stanzas in the case of *Vǫluspá* and *Hávamál*. The volume is subtitled 'A Selection', and contains the Codex Regius mythological poems, *Helreið Brynhildar* and *Vǫlundarkviða* from the heroic poems, and, most unusually, 'Innsteinnsljóð' from *Hálfs saga*, as well as *Eiríksmál* and 'The Waking of Angantýr'. Auden died in 1973; in 1981 Paul Taylor reissued the 1969 volume with twenty-three further versions of eddic poetry by Auden (Auden and Taylor 1981). The volume now included all the heroic poetry from the Codex Regius, 'Hjálmar's Death-Song', 'Hildebrand's Death-Song', 'Hlǫðskviða', the Riddles of Gestumblindi from *Hervarar saga ok Heiðreks*, and *Sólarljóð*. Some poems, such as *Atlamál*, *Sigurðarkviða in skamma*, and *Grípisspá* are scarcely versified, but remain as stanza-by-stanza translations into prose; the other additions are substantial poetic versions. Now that Auden is dead, Taylor pays warm tribute to his qualities as poet in the Foreword: 'He went to the Icelandic itself. I gave him my translations in the best poetic line I could manage, and he turned that verbal and metrical disarray into poetic garb. The product is his' (Auden and Taylor 1981, x).

Terry translates all the Codex Regius poems, plus *Baldrs draumar*, *Grottasǫngr*, and 'The Waking of Angantýr'; *Rígsþula* and *Hyndloljóð* are rejected on the basis of inferior quality. Terry notes the lyrical qualities of the poems, but eschews imitation of the metre, beyond trying 'to suggest, if not reproduce the alliteration' (Terry 1969, ix). She hopes to avoid the pitfalls of Hollander's diction: 'Apart from such embellishments (kennings), the language of the Edda is simple and free from archaisms; I have tried to keep mine the same' (Terry 1969, x). In the same year again, the first volume of Ursula Dronke's edition of the *Poetic Edda* was published (Dronke 1969). This contained important facing-page translations of the last four heroic poems in the Codex Regius (*Atlakviða*, *Atlamál*, *Guðrúnarhvǫt*, and *Hamðismál*). Volume II (1997) contains *Vǫluspá*, *Rígsþula*, *Vǫlundarkviða*, *Lokasenna*, and *Skírnismál*. Auden may have looked at volume I. By 1969 he was beginning to think about moving back to Oxford, and his former college, Christ Church, where he indeed lived for the last year of his life, was also the college of Gabriel Turville-Petre, then Vigfusson Reader in Ancient Icelandic Literature and Antiquities. It seems plausible that Turville-Petre would have brought Dronke's book to Auden's attention. If he saw it, though, he did not pay much attention to the commentary or apparatus: he might otherwise have avoided such misinterpretations as, for example, *Guðrúnarhvǫt* st. 5, which he takes as referring proleptically to the deaths of Hamðir and Sǫrli, rather than back to the deaths of Erpr and Eitill.

My translation appeared in 1996. I included all the texts edited in Neckel and Kuhn 1962, except for 'The Battle of the Goths and Huns', 'Hildebrand's Death-Song', and some eddic fragments, poems which would have demanded too much contextualization and explanation to justify their inclusion. Like Auden and Taylor, I made no statement about my aims in the translation, beyond discussing metre. My implied reader was the ordinary reader, the regular buyer of World's Classics translations, who did not need a translation which reflected every subjunctive or plural-for-singular usage, but who was interested primarily in the narrative and who would appreciate the humour, grandeur, horror, and suspense of the Norse originals.

Translators and Style

In comparison with the 'impenetrable obscurity' of skaldic verse, in Herbert's phrase, the language of the *Poetic Edda* is not particularly difficult to construe, although there are a number of *hapax legomena*, and some passages which are obscure in their reference or damaged in transmission. The poems' narratives can be broadly understood with the help of Snorri (though of course Snorri's interpretations cannot be regarded as definitive). There are few kennings or complex metaphors. Early translators, as we have seen, were constrained by the serial and slow publication of the three volumes of the Copenhagen *Edda*. By the time Thorpe came to make his version, the German philological revolution meant that a better understanding of Old Norse, and a scholarly edition with useful apparatus, were available to him. Bellows uses Hildebrand's 1876 edition, revised by Gering in 1904, but consults the numerous commentaries which had by then appeared. Hollander follows Bugge (1867), while subsequent translators have used Neckel and Kuhn's fourth edition of 1962, with the additions outlined above.[2]

Once the canon has been identified, the translator must decide which, if any, verse form should be employed. Rhyming verse is favoured by Cottle and Herbert; Cottle tends to expand each individual Norse line into at least a couplet. Later translators prefer longer or shorter lines of prose, sometimes arranged as verse, or free verse, either imitating the half-line structure in rhythmic terms, or expanding it further. They must also decide how far the alliteration of the original is to be imitated. This will throw up the problem of the relative lack of synonyms in English, and invites the use of Latinate words or archaisms to fill the gap. The adoption of rhyming couplets is not always successful. Cottle's verse sometimes gives a nicely epigrammatic turn to the eddic line: 'Remember once your hand was bit / By Fenrir in an angry fit' (1797, 163) perhaps trivialises *Ls* 38, but there is some grandeur to the latter part of Skírnir's curse in *Skm* 36 (Cottle 1797, 95):

> Mark the giant ! Mark him well!
> Hear me his attendants tell!
> Can'st thou with the fiends engage,
> Madness, Impotence and Rage?
> Thus thy torments I describe
> The furies in my breast subside.

Internal rhyme can often be effective; Bray's 'quivering and shivering' in *Þrk* 1 is a striking example (1908, 127). The temptation to reproduce exactly the Norse alliteration may produce over-emphatic lines: Auden and Taylor's 'broken to bits was the Brising necklace' in *Þrk* 13 is probably excessive, as well as going beyond the original (1969, 85). The list from *Skm* 36, in the original *ergi, œði ok ópola*, produces a range

---

[2] In the discussion which follows, poem titles are abbreviated according to the scheme used in Neckel and Kuhn 1962.

of possible afflictions for Gerðr: from the gloriously personified 'Madness, Impotence and Rage' of Cottle (1797, 95), who fails to note that these are runic staves rather than demonic powers, to the intensively alliterating 'lechery, loathing and lust' in Hollander (1962, 72), who loses the implication of madness. Bellows gives 'longing, madness, and lust' (1926, 118), Terry, 'frenzy, lewdness and lust' (1969, 59) while 'filth, frenzy and lust' is the choice of Auden and Taylor (1969, 123). Larrington's 'lewdness, frenzy and unbearable desire' makes explicit the connection of *óþola* to its root, *þola* 'to bear with or suffer' (1996, 67), as does Dronke's 'lust', 'burning' and 'unbearable need' (1997, 384). Thorpe keeps the words in their Icelandic forms, accentuating their strangeness by keeping the Icelandic orthography: 'ergi, and œði, and óþoli' (Thorpe 1866, 83).

Bellows is particularly concerned with retaining the rhythm of the different metres, the characteristics of which he describes in detail (1926, xxiii–xxvi), an effort which Terry explicitly eschews. Rhythm is a strong point of Auden and Taylor's work; their substantial discussion of it in the 1969 introduction perhaps reflects the keen ear of Auden as a practising poet. Their version of the curse (*Skm* 35) has a pounding, hypnotic beat (1969, 123):

> Hrimgrimnir shall have you, the hideous troll,
> Beside the doors of the dead,
> Under the tree-roots ugly scullions
> Pour you the piss of goats;
> Nothing else shall you ever drink,
> Never what you wish,
> Ever what I wish.
> I score troll-runes, then I score three letters,
> Filth, frenzy, lust:
> I can score them off as I score them on,
> If I find sufficient cause.

The greatest temptation for the translator is to employ archaisms or etymologize; for Cottle, Herbert, Thorpe, and Vigfusson, 'thou' and 'thee' naturally seem less archaic than they do to twentieth-century translators. *Mær/mey* encourages 'maiden' for 'girl' by assonance and alliteration. The late nineteenth century brings a heightened philological awareness. Typical is Magnússon and Morris's rendition of *Fm* 66: 'Seldom hath hardy eld a faint-heart youth', or *Fm* 211: 'Such as thy redes are I will nowise do after them' (Magnússon and Morris 1870, 61, 62). Vigfusson and York Powell, despite their scathing remarks about the 'mere philologist', enthusiastically render Norse words with their English cognates, or coin philologically possible but unattested words, e.g. 'Anses' for Æsir, and 'Ansesses' for *Ásynjor*, 'Tew' for Týr, 'Eager' for Ægir, and Woden instead of Óðinn, as well as 'bearsarks'; a spelling which commits them to a particular understanding of the ferocious warriors' behaviour. They also use 'methinks' and 'wight'. Bray has the archaic 'ye', as well as 'ween', 'olden', 'twain', the dialectal 'bairns', and not only 'Wanes' for Vanir, but the not entirely happy 'Wanelings' for *vaningja*. Hollander's literalism and etymologizing instinct brings 'fain', 'I ween', and 'I wot', as well as lines such as 'if I wend with thee to the world of etins'; Bellows has 'methinks', 'fare' for 'journey', and 'doth', though he has few other '-th' endings in the present third person singular. Dronke generally captures a modern-sounding idiom, though the demands of alliteration produce the obscure 'Bayard and bracelets' for *iós ok armbauga* in *Ls* 13, more prosaically 'horse and arm-rings' (1997, 336). Bayard is a generic Middle English term for a well-bred horse. Even Auden and Taylor, whose translations usually sound reasonably contemporary, employ 'thurse', 'maids', 'mighty-thewed', and refer to 'garths', 'Vanes' (for Vanir), and 'orcs'. The latter may likely be ascribed to Tolkien's influence—the volume is dedicated to him. 'Busk yourself Freyia' demands Loki in Auden and Taylor, recalling Herbert's 'Now, Freyia, busk, as a blooming bride' (Herbert 1842, 176)—a usage which even in 1804 occasioned an explanatory note.

The problem of synonyms, if not solved by archaisms, leads to a repetition of 'warrior', 'fighter', 'hero' which is almost unavoidable. The etymological attraction of 'mare' for *marr* 'horse' in Auden and Taylor puts Skírnir on an animal whose connotations of effeminacy should have given Auden's expert advisers pause for thought; 'mare' is frequently used elsewhere in their translations. Fighting, of which there is a great deal, entails 'smiting', 'slaying', and 'felling' in Thorpe, Vigfusson and York Powell, Bray, Bellows, and Hollander; Terry prefers 'strike' and 'lay low', while Auden and Taylor alternate between 'fell', 'kill', and 'lay low'. I used 'strike', 'batter', and 'kill'; 'batter' may be too colloquial and perhaps not forceful enough.

Cottle shows no sensitivity to the question of the appropriateness of Latinate or Romance diction: Þrymr's sister, for example, becomes a 'sordid dame'. Herbert makes a point of avoiding Latin-derived words where he can, though he etymologizes freely in his Introduction. Failing to identify the 'Thursar' as giants, he connects them with Turks, Tuscans, *thus* (Latin, 'incense'), and, splendidly, those 'murderous immolators of the East', the Thugs (1842, 187, n.). As a philologist Thorpe is aware that

Latinisms are not appropriate, but he fails to avoid 'compotation' and 'celestial' in *Hym* 1 and uses such terminology as 'Fafnicide' and 'altercation' in poem titles; the jingle of 'Œgir's Compotation, or: Loki's Altercation' must indeed have been hard to resist for *Lokasenna*. There is less Latinism in twentieth-century translation, though Dronke has 'itemize' for *telia* 'reckon up' in *Ls* 28 (1997, 339); the frequently-repeated charge against Loki in this poem that he is *œrr* 'mad', she renders as 'lunatic'.

The language of romance is also difficult: women and girls become 'damsels', 'wenches', 'that fair', or the rather uncourtly 'lass' in Thorpe. Auden and Taylor have 'maids', and Terry 'maidens'; I tried to keep the maidens out, preferring 'girl'. The sexual encounter in *Hrbl* 30 is euphemized into 'sweet colloquy' (Cottle 1797, 116), 'trysting' (Bray 1908, 193), 'dallied' (Thorpe 1866, 76), or 'granted me joy' (Bellows 1926, 131). The same verse's *línhvít* 'linen-white' is assimilated to mid-Victorian ideas of decorum in descriptions of female beauty by Thorpe in 'lily-fair'; Bray gives 'linen-fair', potentially rather puzzling; Hollander loses the comparison by glossing 'white-armed', followed by Terry, while Vigfusson and York Powell, Bellows, Auden and Taylor, and Larrington stick to the literal 'linen-white'. Sex will always raise difficulties; incestuous sex is even trickier. When Freyja is accused of having sex with her brother in *Ls* 32, Cottle completely misunderstands the charge, suggesting that Freyja has orchestrated 'mortal strife' against her brother (1797, 160). Thorpe coyly gives 'against thy brother the gentle powers excited' (1866, 95), while Vigfusson obscures Loki's words with an ellipsis (1883, 105). Hollander converts Loki's charge that Freyja is a witch (*fordæða*) into the accusation that she is a whore (1962, 97); Bray has the gods find her 'at thy brother's' as if she were merely visiting for tea and has her 'frightened' rather than farting (1908, 257). The fart that results when Freyja is discovered *in flagrante* with her brother is first noted by Bellows (1926, 162): 'Freyja her wind set free'; Hollander is the first to translate the fart directly.

Scatology predictably causes problems. *Skm* 35's *geita hland* is 'urine of the unsav'ry goat' for Cottle (1797, 95); 'foul beverage from the goats' is Herbert's version (1842, 201). Thorpe gives 'goat's water' (1866, 83); Vigfusson and York Powell omit the phrase. Bray's 'foul water of goats' (1908, 151), like Herbert's and Thorpe's term, leaves it unclear as to whether the liquid is left-over goats' drinking-water. Hollander's impressive 'staling of stinking goats' depends on the reader recognizing the archaic 'staling' (1962, 72). Bellows's 'horns of filth' misses the link with Heiðrún, the mead-giving goat of Valhǫll (1926, 118). By the sixties 'piss' becomes possible; thus Terry (169, 59), Auden and Taylor (1969, 123), and Larrington (1996, 66); Dronke has the politer 'goat's urine' (1997, 384).

The daughters of Hymir (probably personifications of the mountain rivers flowing into the sea) are mentioned in Loki's insult in *Ls* 34 as urinating in Njǫrðr's mouth. This proves too much for Cottle: 'The sentiments and expressions of this and the following verse would not admit with propriety of an English version' (1797, 161). Thorpe gives the mysterious 'had thee for a utensil' and apologizes: 'the events related in this strophe are probably a mere perversion, by the poet, of what we know of Niörd's history' (1866, I 96); Vigfusson employs an ellipsis; Bray's 'used thee as trough for their floods' is rather vague (1908, 259), while Hollander's 'pot' and 'midden' suggests a product which is too solid (1962, 97); Bellows's 'privy' is more to the point (1926, 63). Terry (1969, 81) and Auden and Taylor (1969, 138) have the coy 'made water in your mouth' while Larrington gives a perhaps dysphemic 'piss-pot' and 'pissed' (1996, 90); Dronke has the etymologically related 'piss-trough', but also 'made water into your mouth' (1997, 340).

Insult is hard too: *Hrbl* 49's *halr inn hugblauði* is literally if unimaginatively rendered 'shameless coward' and 'coward' by Auden and Taylor (1969, 131), and Larrington (1996, 49), respectively. Bellows's 'witless man' loses the connection with courage (1926, 135); Terry's 'faint-hearted fellow' (1969, 66) is, like Bray's 'faint-heart' (1908, 197), perhaps not strong enough. It is the older translators who excel here: Hollander's 'craven knave' (1962, 81) and Thorpe's 'dastardly varlet' (1866, 77) with their internal rhymes, or Cottle's marvellous, if very free 'infernal caitiff, wretch absurd!' (1797, 121).

Some translators seize the opportunity for a witty idiomatic rendering. In *Þrk* 32 Þrymr's sister, who has expected good-will gifts from her new sister-in-law, receives a blow from Mjǫllnir, Þórr's hammer, instead. *Hon scell um hlaut fyr scillinga* tempts some translators to try to reproduce the jingle of *scell* and *scillinga*. Vigfusson and York Powell do rather well with 'she got a pound instead of pence' (1883, 180); Thorpe's 'she a blow got instead of skillings' is confused by the archaism (1866, 66). Bray and Bellows combine 'stroke' and 'shillings' for a near-alliterative effect, but suggesting perhaps a friendly pat on the head (1908, 137; 1926, 182). Hollander has 'shock' and 'shillings' (1962, 108). 'Blow' and 'money' in Terry (1969, 92) and 'blow' and 'gold' in Auden and Taylor (1969, 88) miss the pun, which I tried to render with 'striking' and 'shillings' (1996, 101). Now that 'shillings' are no longer current, the joke will probably disappear.

Though a relatively simple poem in terms of lexis, *Þrymskviða* provides a range of challenges to the translator. In the first stanza there is much emphasis on Þórr's hair and beard; the mysterious loss of his hammer is experienced by the god as uncanny and literally hair-raising in its implications: *scegg nam at hrista, scǫr nam at dýia*. Cottle's version is, as ever, over the top: 'From his heaving breast uprear'd, / Gusty whirlwinds shake his beard' (1797, 179). Bray's 'quivering and shivering' (1908, 127), as noted above, is effective, while Hollander's 'shaggy head gan shake' suggests a certain wobbliness (1962, 104). Bellows (1926, 174–75) and Terry (1969, 88) understand the implications, but Auden and Taylor's 'tossed his red locks', not only makes Þórr sound a little petulant, it also imports the idea of redness, which is attested only for Þórr's beard (1969, 84). In stanza 13, problems of divine dignity are encountered. That Freyja is angry (*reið*) at the suggestion that she should go to Jǫtunheimr to marry Þrymr produces 'wrath' in Herbert, Thorpe, and Vigfusson and York Powell (1842, 176; 1866, 63; 1883, 177); Cottle as usual expands mightily: 'Passion in Freya's cheek glowed hot / Cold tremors thro' her bosom shot' (1797, 184). Freyja's undignified snorting (*fnásaði*) is first recognized by Vigfusson and York Powell. Bray has her panting (1908, 131), while Hollander (1962, 106) reports that she 'foamed with rage' (perhaps even less dignified than snorting). When Freyja refuses on the grounds that going to Jǫtunheimr would prove her to be *vergjarnasta* 'most eager for men', Cottle (1797, 185) falls into the startling error of having her agree to the journey, a consent which, as Herbert tartly remarks, 'destroys the sense of all that follows' (1842, 180). Herbert himself settles on 'wanton bride' as a translation (1842, 176), while Thorpe gives 'lewedest' (1866, 64). Vigfusson and York Powell have the literal 'man-maddest' (1883, 178), varied by Hollander as 'most mad after men' (1962, 106). Bray's 'most wanton' and Bellows's 'most lustful' are quite neutral (1908, 131; 1926, 177). Terry (1969, 90) spells out 'I'll have gone mad with hunger for men', while Auden and Taylor (1969, 85) too directly make Freyja a 'whore', losing the superlative which is an important part of the comedy, for Freyja fears to prove herself an outstanding example of what she already is. My own 'most sex-crazed of women', I now think likely to date (1996, 98).

Thus far I have mostly considered the mythological poetry, since the earliest translators were most interested in the mythological parallels with the Greek. Particular interest in the heroic poetry was probably kindled by the work of Magnússon and Morris, reinforced no doubt by the first performance of Wagner's Ring Cycle in London in May 1882. It is interesting to compare the versions of Magnússon and Morris, Auden's 1981 texts and Dronke's translations of the last four heroic poems. The Victorian translators strive more for effect than for clarity; Auden is oddly literal and unpoetic in these last versions, while Dronke very often finds the *mot juste*, creating a series of images which are coherent in their implications. Space permits only one example: three versions of *Hm* 20, chronicling the arrogant reaction of Jǫrmunrekkr to the news that Hamðir and Sǫrli have arrived at his hall. The verse lists a sequence of the king's self-conscious actions (Neckel and Kuhn 1962, 272):

> Hló þá Iǫrmunreccr, hendi drap á kampa,
> beiddiz at brǫngo, bǫðvaðiz at víni;
> scóc hann scǫr iarpa, sá á sciǫld hvítan,
> lét hann sér í hendi hvarfa ker gullit.

> Loud Jormunrek laughed,
> And laid hand to his beard,
> Nor bade bring his byrny,
> But with the wine fighting,
> Shook his red locks,
> On his white shield sat staring,
> And in his hand
> Swung the gold cup on high
>   (Magnússon and Morris 1870, 255–56).

> Then Iǫrmunrekkr laughed,
> with his hand stroked his whiskers,
> spurred himself to wildness,
> grew battlesome over his wine,
> flung back his brown hair,
> glanced at his white shield,
> made the golden cup
> swing in his hand.
>   (Dronke 1969, 165).

> The stout-hearted king stroked his beard,
> And laughed grimly, aggressive from wine;
> He shook his locks, looked at his shield,
> And twirled the golden goblet he held.
>   (Auden and Taylor 1981, 142).

Magnússon and Morris add elements not present in the Norse: loudness of laughter, a byrnie, redness to the hair; they muddy the relationship between the wine and the fighting and break the rhythm of the series of speedy actions by making Jǫrmunrekkr sit and stare, as if preoccupied, at his shield, while at the same time he swings his cup. Dronke nicely captures the studiedness of Jǫrmunrekkr's behaviour without recourse to archaism, except perhaps in 'battlesome'; the lexis is simple: 'cup', 'brown', 'white'. The 'whiskers', a description of facial hair which at the same time evokes an alert animal, is better than 'beard'. She keeps the swiftness of the successive gestures with 'glance', suggesting a fleeting awareness that he may indeed have to fight in person, and making the cup casually 'swing in the hand' underlines the self-consciousness of the king, the focus of all attention in the hall. Auden's 'stout-hearted', there for the alliteration, is too conventional to be effective; though 'aggressive' captures the sense of *bǫðvaðiz* quite well and echoes 'grimly', it lacks the element of working himself up to fury which the Norse reflexives convey, and which Dronke retains in 'spurred himself'. 'Locks' again alliterates, but at the cost of archaism; the series of colours, 'brown', 'white', 'golden', is lost, and the 'twirling', though studiedly negligent, seems rather dainty for the leader of the Goths. Comparing the three verses shows the compromises in subtlety which faithfulness to alliteration can demand; Magnússon and Morris lack the precision which Dronke manages, though they have a strong sense of rhythm—perhaps stronger than Auden's here.

Beyond problems of tone and diction, translators must decide what to do with Norse names, whether occurring singly or in the great lists of *Grímnismál* or the *Dvergatal* of *Vǫluspá*, the varying status of which, as Quinn comments, 'has the dwarfs being marched in and out of the poem throughout the last hundred or so years' (1994, 127). Some translators, such as Thorpe and Terry, keep the *Grímnismál* catalogue in its Norse form; Vigfusson and York Powell make a start on listing the names in stanza 46, then abandon the list with 'etc'. Auden and Taylor and I chose to mix the translation of the more perspicuous names with the retention in the original form of those whose meaning is obscure. Hollander (1962, xxix) comments sagely that the matter

> presents a knotty problem to the translator. [...] I do not hesitate to say that on the translator's tact and skill in meeting this problem—for dodge it he cannot—will depend in large measure the artistic merit of his work and its modicum of palatableness to the modern reader.

Dronke gamely translates all the dwarf-names of *Vǫluspá*, in places guessing at possible etymologies, so that *Nóri* becomes 'Shipper'. Ingeniously she manages to keep some of the internal rhymes: *Skirvir* and *Virvir* become 'Joiner' and 'Groiner', though this also results in 'Trembler' and 'Trumbler' (a nonce word) for *Bivǫrr* and *Bavǫrr* (1997, 9–11). The replacement of unfamiliar with familiar name forms can have unfortunate, even hilarious, results. Quinn has noted the unaccountable decision of Auden and Taylor to begin their version of *Vǫluspá* by re-christening the *seiðkona* Heiðr with the name of the Swiss goat-girl Heidi (Quinn 1994, 128).

Translators have also to make decisions about the fidelity with which they render word order. The Norse case system allows inversion of subject and object as modern English does not; confusion can sometimes arise when the Norse syntax is imitated too literally. Thorpe keeps the Norse word order for the final line of *Þrymskviða* quite successfully: 'So got Odin's son his hammer back' (1866, 66), but Hollander's 'Laughed Hlórrithi's heart within him / when the hammer beheld the hardy one' runs the risk of personifying Miǫllnir (1962, 108). Vigfusson and York Powell opt for 'This is how Woden's son got back his Hammer' (1883, 180). Terry keeps the inversion but makes it sound natural, 'That's how the hammer came back to Thor's hands' (1969, 92). 'Thus Thor came to recover his hammer' (Auden and Taylor 1969, 88) alliterates, where Larrington 'So Odin's son got the hammer back' is strictly literal (1996, 101).

Understanding of Norse religious practices tests translators, nowhere more than in *Hym* 1, a truly difficult verse for those who have not immersed themselves in 'the old life' as Vigfusson and York Powell call it (1883, cxiv). Cottle has the gods examining entrails like classical soothsayers, 'Till the teeming entrails tell, / Truth divin'd by mistic spell' (1797, 127). Thorpe's bald 'rods they shook' leaves the divination highly mysterious and he fails to register that Ægir does have some kettles (1866, 56). Vigfusson and York Powell's 'they cast the divining rods, and inspected the blood' (1883, 220), and Bray's 'they shook divining twigs, scanned the blood-drops' (1908, 113) make the process admirably clear, though Bray's vision of the gods eating 'dainties' seems rather effetely delicate. Hollander's 'on wassail bent their wands they shook' complicates by use of archaism (1962, 83), while Bellows's 'blood they tried' makes it sound as if the gods are drinking the substance (1926, 139), as does Auden and Taylor's 'relished blood' (1969, 89). The latter also elaborate the divination-twigs as rune-carving on wood, which is not what the text says. Terry's 'by shaking small branches, steeped in blood' may be over-explanatory, but her translation is probably clearer than mine: 'they shook the twigs and looked at the augury' (1996, 78).

The translator's task will always be fraught with anxieties. 'At best his version is to the original as the thin, muffled, meagre, telephone-rendering is to the full rich tones which it transmits, faithfully, it is true, but with what a difference to the hearer!' exclaim Vigfusson and York Powell (1883, cxvi). Translations are not for all time, but simply for their own particular age, 'a stop-gap until made to give place to a worthier work' as Thorpe modestly observes (1866, I viii). Translators ought to articulate to themselves and to their readers what prejudices and predilections they bring to the project. As a teacher of Old Norse, I felt clarity was more important than poetic effect in my translation, though every now and again I rewarded myself with a little *jeu d'esprit*. It is both salutary and educational to read earlier versions: translators generally hope that their versions will stand the test of time, but through their ideas of appropriate diction, whether the lofty Latinisms of Cottle's late eighteenth-century Gothic, the more subdued romanticism of Herbert, the simplicity of Thorpe, the coyness of Bray, the 'Teutonic ambience' of Bellows, the archaisms of Hollander in pursuit of his sound effects, the free additions in Auden and Taylor, and the occasional jaunty sixties note of Terry, each translator inevitably imparts a flavour of the contemporary.

Bibliography

Auden, W. H., Paul B. Taylor and Peter H. Salus, trans., 1969. *The Elder Edda: A Selection.*
Auden, W. H. and Paul B. Taylor, trans., 1981. *Norse Poems.*
Bartholin[us], Thomas 1689. *Antiquitatum Danicarum de causis contemptae a Danis adhuc gentilibus mortis.*
Bellows, Henry A., trans., [1923] 1926. *The Poetic Edda.* (Single-volume reprint).
Bellows, Henry A., trans., [1923] 1991. *The Poetic Edda.* Reprinted with introduction by William O. Cord.
Bennett, J. A. W. 1938. 'The History of Old English and Old Norse Studies in England from the time of Francis Junius till the End of the Eighteenth Century'. Unpublished doctoral dissertation. University of Oxford.
Bray, Olive, ed. and trans., 1908. *The Elder or Poetic Edda.*
Bugge, Sophus, ed., 1867. *Norrœn fornkvædi: islandsk samling af folkelige oldtidsdigte . . . Sæmundar Edda hins fróða.*
Clunies Ross, Margaret 1998. *The Norse Muse in Britain 1750–1820.*
Clunies Ross, Margaret 2001. *The Old Norse Poetic Translations of Thomas Percy: A New Edition and Commentary.*
Cottle, Amos, trans., 1797. *Icelandic Poetry, or the Edda of Sæmund.*
Dronke, Ursula, ed. and trans., 1969. *The Poetic Edda: Volume I. Heroic poems.*
Dronke, Ursula, ed. and trans., 1997. *The Poetic Edda: Volume II. Mythological Poems.*
Edda Sæmundar hinns fróda 1787, 1818, 1828. Ed. Arnamagnaean Commission. 3 vols.

Gray, Thomas 1768. *Poems by Mr. Gray.*
Herbert, William, trans., 1804. *Select Icelandic Poetry: Translated from the Originals with Notes. Part First.*
Herbert, William, trans., 1806. *Select Icelandic Poetry: Translated from the Originals with Notes. Part Second.*
Herbert, William 1842. *Works of the Hon. And Very Rev. William Herbert, Dean of Manchester etc. Excepting those on Botany and Natural History; with Additions and Corrections by the Author.* 3 vols. Vol. 1 contains *Horae Scandicae: Or, Works Relating to Old Scandinavian Literature: Select Icelandic Poetry : Translated from the Originals with Notes; Revised with Three Additional Pieces from Sæmund's Edda.*
Hildebrand, Karl, ed., [1876] 1904. *Die Lieder der Älteren Edda.* 2nd edn, rev. Hugo Gering.
Hollander, Lee M., trans., 1928. *The Poetic Edda.*
Hollander, Lee M., trans., 1936. *Old Norse Poems.*
Hollander, Lee M., trans., 1962. *The Poetic Edda.* 2nd rev. edn.
La Farge, Beatrice and John Tucker, eds., 1992. *Glossary to the Poetic Edda: Based on Hans Kuhn's Kurzes Wörterbuch.*
Larrington, Carolyne, trans., 1996. *The Poetic Edda: A New Translation.*
Lassen, Annette 2006. 'Hrafnagaldur Óðins / Forspjallsljóð: et antikvariskt dikt?' In *The Fantastic in Old Norse/Icelandic Literature. Sagas and the British Isles.* Preprint papers of the Thirteenth International Saga Conference, Durham and York 6th–12th August 2006. Ed. John McKinnell, David Ashurst, and Donata Kick, 551–60.
Lüning, Hermann, ed., 1859. *Die Edda: eine Sammlung altnordischer Götter- und Heldenlieder.*
Macpherson, James 1771. *An Introduction to the History of Great Britain and Ireland.*
Magnússon, Eiríkr and William Morris, trans., 1870. *Völsunga saga: the Story of the Volsungs & Niblungs, with Certain Songs from the Elder Edda.*
Mallet, Paul Henri 1755. *Introduction à l'histoire de Dannemarc: où l'on traite de la religion, des loix, des mœurs & des usages des anciens Danois.* 6 vols.
Mallet, Paul Henri 1756. *Monumens de la mythologie et de la poésie des Celtes, et particulièrement des anciens Scandinaves: pour servir de supplément et de preuves à l'Introduction à l'histoire de Dannemarc.* 6 vols.
Neckel, Gustav, ed., 1962. *Edda. Die Lieder des Codex Regius nebst verwandten Denkmälern.* 4th edn, rev. Hans Kuhn.
Percy, Thomas, trans., 1763. *Five Pieces of Runic Poetry from the Icelandic Language.*
Percy, Thomas 1770. *Northern Antiquities.*
Pratt, Lynda 1994. 'The Southey Circle and Scandinavian Mythology and Literature'. In *Celtic and Germanic Themes in European Literature.* Ed. Neil Thomas, 95–107.
Quinn, Judy 1994. 'Vǫluspá in Twentieth-Century Scholarship in English'. In *Old Norse Studies in the New World: A Collection of Essays to Celebrate the*

Jubilee of the Teaching of Old Norse at the University of Sydney 1943–1993. Ed. Geraldine Barnes, Margaret Clunies Ross, and Judy Quinn, 120–37.

Quinn, Judy and Margaret Clunies Ross 1994. 'The Image of Norse Poetry and Myth in Seventeenth-Century England'. In *Northern Antiquity: The Post-Medieval Reception of Edda and Saga*. Ed. Andrew Wawn, 189–210.

Ranisch, Wilhelm and Andreas Heusler, eds, 1903. *Eddica minora: Dichtungen eddischer Art aus den Fornaldarsögur und anderen Prosawerken*.

Rask, Rasmus, ed., 1818. *Snorra-Edda ásamt skáldu og þarmeð fylgjandi ritgjörðum, eptir gömlum skinnbókum*.

Resen, Peder Hans, ed., 1665. *Edda Islandorum*.

Sammes, Aylett 1676. *Britannia antiqua illustrata; or the Antiquities of Antient Britain*.

Sheringham, Robert 1670. *De Anglorum gentis origine disceptatio*.

Terry, Patricia, trans., 1969. *Poems of the Vikings: The Elder Edda*.

Thorpe, Benjamin, trans., 1866. *Edda Sæmundar hinns fróða: The Edda of Sæmund the Learned*.

Vigfusson, Gudbrand and Frederick York Powell, eds and trans., 1883. *Corpus Poeticum Boreale. The Poetry of the Old Northern Tongue from the Earliest Times to the Thirteenth Century*. Vol. 1 *Eddic Poetry*.

Wawn, Andrew 2000. *The Vikings and the Victorians: Inventing the Old North in Nineteenth-century Britain*.

WILLIAM MORRIS AND THE VOLSUNGS

DAVID ASHURST

William Morris's interest in the Old North is already evident in his first publications, the pieces that he contributed, at twenty-two years of age, to *The Oxford and Cambridge Magazine*, which appeared at intervals during 1856. At this point in his life, when he had recently graduated from the University of Oxford, Morris was a competent reader of Latin, Greek, and French but his knowledge of Old Norse-Icelandic literature and culture was secondhand and limited in scope. The Scandinavian materials available in English were relatively scarce at this date but those that Morris encountered clearly caught his imagination, as he himself declares in the apparently autobiographical, though possibly fictive, preamble to the *Magazine* story called 'Lindenborg Pool' (Morris 1910–15 (hereafter *Works*), I 245):

> I read once in lazy humour Thorpe's Northern Mythology,[1] on a cold May night when the north wind was blowing; in lazy humour, but when I came to the tale that is here amplified there was something in it that fixed my attention and made me think of it; and whether I would or no, my thoughts ran in this way, as here follows. So I felt obliged to write, and wrote accordingly.

In this passage the phrase 'the tale that is here amplified' is particularly significant because it announces the literary approach that would be Morris's chief *modus operandi* as a poet during the next two decades, which culminated in the publication, in 1876, of *The Story of Sigurd and the Fall of the Niblungs* (*Works* XII), a work that for many an admirer of Morris is quite simply 'the greatest of all his poems' (Paul Thompson 1977, 200) and which is based closely on *Vǫlsunga saga* and parts of the *Poetic Edda* with a few elements taken from the *Nibelungenlied*. For Morris in these decades, as for the medieval authors to whom he felt closest, the act of literary creation was primarily and unabashedly one of re-creation, of refashioning received material.

Malory and Froissart are the chief sources for the items in Morris's first book of poetry, *The Defence of Guenevere and Other Poems*, which was published in 1858 (*Works* I). This collection contains some of Morris's

---

[1] Thorpe 1851–52. In addition to 'Lindenborg Pool', two other of the eight *Magazine* tales have Scandinavian content with medieval settings.

most frequently anthologized works but the poems in it, with their concentrated expression and their evocative but sometimes puzzling allusiveness, are not representative of his more mature style, in which he is characteristically expansive and at pains to elucidate whatever he thinks the reader needs to know.

More typical in every way is the next large-scale project that came to fulfilment: *The Earthly Paradise* (*Works* III–VI).[2] This is a huge compilation of twenty-four stories in verse, originally published in three volumes (1868–70), with a framing narrative in which a group of voyagers, referred to in the Argument of the Prologue (*Works*, III 3) as 'certain gentlemen and mariners of Norway', flee the Black Death in the fourteenth century and go in search of the Earthly Paradise, partly encouraged in this venture by stories of the Greenlanders' discovery of Vineland (13); instead of Paradise, however, they come at last to an unknown island where the inhabitants are, as they put it, 'the seed of the Ionian race' (5), i.e. descendants of the Greeks; there they are made welcome and agree, at the islanders' suggestion, to hold a gathering twice every month; at each gathering one tale will be told for the sake of entertainment and understanding—first by an islander, then by a voyager, and so on alternately for a year. Hence *The Earthly Paradise* consists of twelve stories that might reasonably be called 'southern', of ancient Greek origin and told by the hosts, alternating with twelve narratives suitable for telling by medieval Scandinavians and their associates. This scheme allows Morris maximum opportunity to range through his favourite types of source material, the Classical, the mainstream medieval European, and the Nordic. In connexion with this, the weighting of material in favour of the Classical sources serves as a reminder that Morris was by no means fixated on 'northernness' despite his growing love for Old Norse literature: towards the end of the 1850s, after publishing the Scandinavian-influenced stories in the *Oxford and Cambridge Magazine* and the predominantly French-influenced pieces in *The Defence of Guenevere*, he worked on a set of dramatic poems now known as 'Scenes from the Fall of Troy' (*Works* XXIV), which he left as fragments; in the 1860s he produced *The Life and Death of Jason* (see note 2) and the Greek-derived stories of *The Earthly Paradise*; immediately before working on *The Story of Sigurd*, at the height of his involvement with Icelandic

---

[2] *The Life and Death of Jason* was published first (1867, *Works* II) but had originally been meant for inclusion in *The Earthly Paradise*. It quickly outgrew its intended context and took on independent life. A success with critics and the public, it was *Jason* that made Morris's name as a poet.

literature, he produced an impressive verse translation of Virgil's *Æneid* (published 1875 but dated 1876, *Works* XI); and in 1887–88 he issued a poetical version of Homer's *Odyssey* (*Works* XIII), of which Oscar Wilde wrote that 'of all our English translations this is the most perfect and the most satisfying' (Faulkner 1973, 302). These works represent an important aspect of Morris's literary output to set beside his achievements as a translator and re-fashioner of Old Norse material.

When Morris began working on *The Earthly Paradise* he still had to rely on secondhand accounts for his northern stories. It seems likely, for example, that he planned and possibly wrote what became the December tale entitled 'The Fostering of Aslaug'—in which the daughter of Sigurðr and Brynhildr is brought up as the thrall of peasants but eventually marries Ragnarr loðbrók—at a time when he was not directly acquainted with either *Vǫlsunga saga* or *Ragnars saga*, and that he adapted the story from the account in Thorpe's *Northern Mythology* (Hodgson 1987, 85, and May Morris's comment in *Works*, VII xxxii). In the autumn of 1868, however, Morris seized the opportunity to improve the state of his knowledge when he was put in touch with the Icelander Eiríkr Magnússon. Eiríkr tells of his first meeting with the poet (printed by May Morris in *Works*, VII xv–xvi): arriving at Morris's residence, he was soon drawn into enthusiastic conversation in which Morris displayed a knowledge of George Dasent's translations of *Njáls saga* and *Gísla saga* (1861 and 1866), Benjamin Thorpe's translation of the *Poetic Edda* (1866), Amos Cottle's *Icelandic Poetry* (1797) and Percy's *Northern Antiquities* (1770 and 1847), also Sir Walter Scott's account of *Eyrbyggja saga* (1814) and several modern travel books about Iceland;[3] Eiríkr was asked to visit three times per week to give translation classes and it was agreed, at his suggestion, that the first work to be tackled would be *Gunnlaugs saga ormstungu*. This was finished in a fortnight, whereupon the two men began work on *Grettis saga*. Eiríkr further explains (xvii) that it was their habit to go through a passage together, with Eiríkr explaining points of grammar so that Morris could learn the subject piecemeal since he was averse to memorizing grammatical paradigms, after which the Icelander would go away and write out a close translation to be delivered at the next meeting; Morris would then go over the passage again at his leisure and put Eiríkr's translation into his own

---

[3] The translators' original preface to *The Story of Grettir the Strong* (*Works* VII, xxxvii) also indicates that Morris had a knowledge, at least by early 1869, of Edmund Head's translation of *Víga-Glúms saga* (1866), Samuel Laing's rendering of *Heimskringla* (1844), and Dasent's version of Snorri's *Edda* (1842).

preferred style. This last point indicates that Morris was intent on publication from the very first, and in fact 'The Saga of Gunnlaug Worm-Tongue' (*Works* X) appeared in *The Fortnightly Review* in January 1869, only a few months after the first meeting, to be followed in May of the same year by *The Story of Grettir the Strong* (*Works* VII), published by F. S. Ellis, who was also at this time issuing *The Earthly Paradise*. Morris and Eiríkr worked in addition on *Laxdœla saga*, but in this case the fruit of their labour did not appear as a joint translation; rather it formed the basis for Morris's poem 'The Lovers of Gudrun', which re-fashions the central story of the saga as something tantamount to a verse novel, and which forms the high point of the final *Earthly Paradise* volume as published in 1870 (*Works* V–VI).

The same year also saw the publication of *Völsunga Saga: The Story of the Volsungs and Niblungs, with Certain Songs from the Elder Edda* (*Works* VII). According to Eiríkr's account of his first meeting with Morris (*Works*, VII xvi), the poet was on that occasion in 1868 'already preoccupied with the grand types of the heroes (Sigurd the Volsung) and heroines (Brynhild, Gudrun) of the Elder Edda', with which he was familiar from Thorpe's translation (Thorpe 1851–52). Like many another reader who approaches *Vǫlsunga saga* itself from this direction, however, Morris seems to have been initially disappointed by it when he finally made its acquaintance in the summer of 1869. At this point he was taking a cure in Bad Ems, though working as ever; here he received Eiríkr's preliminary translation of the saga and wrote a letter home in which he described the saga as 'rather of the monstrous order' (*Works*, VII xx); but it seems he had not made time to read beyond the first part of the story before his return to England. Eiríkr's description of subsequent developments is worth quoting at length (*Works*, VII xx):

> I resumed lessons with him on the old system—three days a week— this time taking the story of the men of Salmonriverdale (Laxdaela). Some time afterwards—I forget how long—when I came for the appointed lesson, I found him in a state of great excitement, pacing his study. He told me he had now finished reading my translation of the 'grandest tale that was ever told.' He would at once set about copying it out, and procure the original for himself, which he promptly did. On my suggesting that it would be desirable for him to go through the originals of the Edda songs on which the story was based, he set aside for a while the Laxdaela Saga and we got to work on the heroic songs of the Edda.

Four points of interest arise from this passage, the first being that Morris eventually found in the saga, or rather in the story underlying it, the grandeur for which his earlier reading of the *Poetic Edda* in translation had caused him to hope. This should be borne in mind when considering the style that he adopted for his translation of the saga; it also has a bearing on the fact, discussed below, that for several years he hesitated over whether he could or should write a poem of his own on the basis of the story. Secondly there is the matter of Morris's 'state of great excitement', surely indicative of a strong personal and emotional involvement with the story and its characters. This connects with the third point, which concerns the role of *Laxdœla saga* in the evolution of Morris's response to the Volsung tale: Eiríkr implies that, having found the poet less impressed with *Vǫlsunga saga* than he had hoped, he suggested working on the Laxdale story; if so, it was a canny move on his part because there is a well recognized though inexact correlation between the central story of *Laxdœla saga*, with its set of love-triangles involving Guðrún, Bolli, Kjartan, and Hrefna, and that of *Vǫlsunga saga*, with Brynhildr, Gunnarr, Sigurðr, and Guðrún, and because the idea of the love-triangle was peculiarly important to Morris. The relationships between Morris, his wife Janey, and his friend Dante Gabriel Rossetti, whatever their exact nature, caused Morris a certain amount of emotional stress during the late 1860s as he suffered jealousy aroused by Janey's involvement with Rossetti and yet to some extent acquiesced in their liaison (MacCarthy 1994, 221–27);[4] his imaginative portrayal of love-triangles had begun much earlier than this, however, for they play a major role in his stories issued in *The Oxford and Cambridge Magazine* in 1856, particularly 'The Story of the Unknown Church' and 'Frank's Sealed Letter' (*Works* I). Even if Eiríkr did not engineer it, therefore, the choice of *Laxdœla saga* as a subject of study was likely, in the long run, to stimulate Morris's interest in the kind of story that lies at the heart of *Vǫlsunga saga*; it certainly did so in the short term, as is shown by the production of 'The Lovers of Gudrun'. Finally it should be noted that Eiríkr's promotion of the lays of the *Poetic Edda*, given that Morris was already predisposed to honour these works, surely encouraged the publication of the translation in the particular form it took, in which several eddic poems have been interpolated in the saga narrative at points where they add to the aesthetic effect.

---

[4] The generosity of Morris's acquiescence in the period immediately after the publication of the *Vǫlsunga saga* translation is shown by the fact that in 1871 he secured Kelmscott Manor on a joint tenancy with Rossetti. As E. P. Thompson (1977, 161) remarks, 'There is no doubt that Morris hoped it would provide a home where Janey and the children could share Rossetti's company during his own absence.'

In connection with the filling out of the text, it should be noted that the preface to *The Story of the Volsungs and Niblungs* indicates an awareness that the saga is less than wholly satisfactory as it stands and that the reader has to make an effort to get beyond the occasional defects in the narrative so as to reach the heart of the matter (*Works*, VII 286):

> As to the literary quality of this work we might say much, but we think we may well trust the reader of poetic insight to break through whatever entanglement of strange matters or unused elements may at first trouble him, and to meet the nature and beauty with which it is filled.

Morris and Eiríkr were determined, therefore, to deliver the tale in a way that would minimize the defects while still acknowledging their existence. Their method does not involve any sleight of hand or deception of the public, for the preface and Eiríkr's endnotes list the translators' interventions clearly and unambiguously, though in the text itself the eddic interpolations are worked in seamlessly so as to improve, or at least not to impede, the narrative flow. The most important of these interpolations are the following: the song of the birds to Sigurðr after he has killed Fáfnir and Reginn, which is taken from *Fáfnismál* 40–44 (eliminating the name Sigrdrífa) and serves to amplify the prose text's all-too-brief mention of Brynhildr as the woman whom Sigurðr should seek and marry (*Works*, VII 332);[5] the verses associated with the waking of Brynhildr, which are taken from the beginning of *Sigrdrífomál* and serve to balance the long passage borrowed from the same poem by the medieval saga writer, as well as to increase the solemnity of the fatal moment when Sigurðr and the valkyrie meet (*Works*, VII 335); and the whole of *Guðrúnarqviða in fyrsta*, which is given a chapter of its own just after Guðrún has declared that her kinsmen have slain her husband, and greatly increases the emotional impact of this climactic part of the narrative (*Works*, VII 366). The preface, furthermore, outlines the points of contact between the saga and the *Poetic Edda*, indicating on each occasion whether the relevant eddic poems have been offered in the appendix if they have not been subsumed into the main text. In short, everything reasonable has been done to give the novice reader a clear idea of the story in its various ramifications as they appear in the saga and the *Poetic Edda* (but not in Snorri's *Edda* or *Þiðreks saga*) and at the same time to provide the fullest, simplest, and most satisfying experience of story-telling. As regards the form of the *Vǫlsunga saga* translation, then, it can be seen that the work is above all that of men

---

[5] All references to eddic poems are to Neckel and Kuhn 1983.

who cared about their material and wanted others to share their enjoyment of it.

It has already been noted that Morris responded to *Vǫlsunga saga* with strong emotion. He articulated this response in a letter to his friend Charles Eliot Norton (quoted by Paul Thompson 1977, 200):

> The scene of the last interview between Sigurd and the despairing and terrible Brynhild touches me more than anything I have ever met with in literature; there is nothing wanting in it, nothing forgotten, nothing repeated, nothing overstrained; all tenderness is shown without the use of a tender word, all misery and despair without a word of raving, complete beauty without an ornament, and all this in two pages of moderate print.

To be touched in similar fashion by the deep but restrained pathos of the saga is what Morris and Eiríkr expected for 'the reader of poetic insight' who would take the trouble to overcome the initial difficulties of the work's strangeness, as they say in their preface (*Works*, VII 286):

> We cannot doubt that such a reader will be intensely touched by finding, amidst all its wildness and remoteness, such startling realism, such subtilty, such close sympathy with all the passions that may move himself to-day.

It is clearly with the intention of heightening the reader's emotional response, as mentioned above, that the translators interpolate *Guðrúnarqviða in fyrsta*, which they say is the 'the most lyrical, the most complete, and the most beautiful of all the Eddaic poems' (285); they add that it is 'a poem that any age or language might count among its most precious possessions'. Though it chiefly portrays the grief of Guðrún, however, they say that they have inserted it 'before the death of the heroine' (285), thus showing that their primary focus is on Brynhildr, as Morris also implies in his verse prologue to the translation (290), when he says that the saga tells

> Of Brynhild's glorious soul with love distraught,
> Of Gudrun's weary wandering unto naught.

The nature of the emotional experience that Morris invites us to enjoy is indicated in the first lines of the same stanza, which issue this exhortation:

> So draw ye round and hearken, English Folk,
> Unto the best tale pity ever wrought!

We are to respond with compassion; and if we are moved to admiration also, for the tale of the Volsungs is 'the grandest tale that was ever told', it must be an admiration that cannot be severed from pity. This, indeed, is the response that Morris asks from us in the lines on 'Iceland First

Seen' (*Works*, IX 126), in which Brynhildr is held up as the emblem of Iceland itself, apostrophized here as the land of bleakness and story:

> For what is the mark on thy brow but the brand that thy Brynhild doth bear?
> Lone once, and loved and undone by a love that no ages outwear.

This combination—of grandeur, of a love that moves one to admiration and pity, and of a story that endures through centuries—should be borne in mind while considering the implications of Morris and Eiríkr's announcement, made in the opening sentence of their preface to the *Vǫlsunga saga* translation (*Works*, VII 283), that what they are offering the reader is 'the great Epic of the North'. In the final paragraph of the same preface they elaborate their meaning (286):

> This is the Great Story of the North, which should be to all our race what the Tale of Troy was to the Greeks—to all our race first, and afterwards, when the change of the world has made our race nothing more than a name of what has been—a story too—then should it be to those that come after us no less than the Tale of Troy has been to us.

Clearly this passage indicates a sense of kindred between all the Germanic peoples of northern Europe, for whom the Volsung story is conceived as providing a common literary bond; in this respect the writers are to some extent aligning themselves with the movement known as pan-Germanism, which exerted so profound an influence on Richard Wagner in his handling of the same material in *Der Ring des Nibelungen* (Árni Björnsson 2003, 68–117). Their remarks, however, should not be understood as indicating a racist chauvinism of the north: in the first place Morris's admiration for the epics of the Mediterranean, discussed above and demonstrated by his translations of Homer and Virgil, shines through the comments about the tale of Troy; in addition, the remarks are striking for the emphasis they put on the fact that 'our race' will in due course become 'nothing more than a name'—except that it will also be a story. If there is any implied satisfaction in the achievements of the northern European peoples, the great imperial powers of the nineteenth century, it is no more than that they will in time become the subject of one story among others. Perhaps one may say 'one epic among others'.

The use of the term 'epic' in the context of the industrial and imperial world of the Victorian age has been problematized by several critics, especially in connection with *The Story of Sigurd*, Morris's own attempt to write a poetic narrative on the subject of 'the great Epic of the North' (see the unsigned article from the *International Review* reprinted in Faulkner 1973, 263–67, and Dentith 1999). Dentith in particular sees it as paradoxical that a poet who was one of the most committed to the values of epic should also have been one of the most admirable critics of the British empire. Morris makes it clear, however, that what he means by epic, in connection with his *Vǫlsunga saga* translation, is radically at odds with the pomp of empire. The verse prologue specifies that 'the North', to which this epic pertains, is primarily represented by Iceland (*Works*, VII 289):

> O hearken, ye who speak the English Tongue,
> How in a waste land ages long ago,
> The very heart of the North bloomed into song
> After long brooding o'er this tale of woe!
> Hearken, and marvel how it might be so.

Far from being an epic of empire and power it is the expression of those who have neither—nor do they have industry or material assets of any kind (289):

> Or rather marvel not, that those should cling
> Unto the thoughts of great lives passed away,
> Whom God has stripped so bare of everything,
> Save the one longing to wear through their day,
> In fearless wise.

It has already been noted that the idea of greatness passing away and becoming a story is crucial to Morris's concept of epic as expressed in the preface; so it is fitting, according to Morris's view of things, that the Great Story of the North should be produced by a people destitute of everything except endurance and the gift of story-telling. Nor is the story that they tell, after long brooding, one that hankers for the power and riches that they lack; rather it is, as the penultimate line of the verse prologue puts it, a tale 'Of utter love defeated utterly' (290). It is an epic of defeat, therefore, and this is exactly what one would expect, according to Morris's view; for the place where the heart of the North bloomed into song is characterized, in 'Iceland First Seen' (*Works*, IX 126), as the land 'of the courage that may not avail, / Of the longing that may not attain, / of the love that shall never forget'—and it is in this context that Brynhildr is taken to be its emblem.

Even though the kind of epic conceived by Morris belongs to the poor and is an epic of defeat, it is nevertheless grand; this fact has consequences for the kind of language to be used in the *Vǫlsunga saga* translation (and in the other translations from Old Norse, though the issue is particularly relevant to this work). The archaic diction and syntax employed by Morris, and the terms he coined on the basis of etymological connections, have always been the focus of criticism: see, for example, the 1870 review written by G. A. Simcox with the help of Guðbrandur Vigfússon (Faulkner 1973, 152–56) and the comments by Eiríkr himself printed in May Morris's introduction to the 1911 edition (*Works*, VII xvii–xix). There are two main objections to Morris's language, the first being that it misrepresents the style of saga prose, which would not have seemed archaic to the audience for which it was written, and the second being that it puts an obstacle in the way of the modern reader who, as Morris and Eiríkr were aware and as discussed above, already has to cope with much strangeness on encountering the narrative. In connection with the first point, however, it should be acknowledged that much saga prose, in the original Old Icelandic, has a peculiar dignity which cannot be reproduced in modern English; a really close translation will inevitably be stiff, choppy, and strange, whilst one in free-flowing colloquial language will miss the lapidary quality of the original and falsify its style just as much as Morris does, though in a different way. Although it is out of fashion, therefore, there is still something to be said for Morris's solution. There is insufficient room here for a full discussion, but the point may be illustrated with an example drawn from the final dialogue between Brynhildr and Sigurðr, which Morris so admired: '*Heldr en þú deyir, vil ek þik eiga, en fyrirláta Guðrúnu,*' *segir Sigurðr, en svá þrútnuðu hans síður at í sundr gengr brynjuhringar* (Finch 1965, 56). Finch's well-respected translation renders this as follows (56): '"Rather than you should die, I'll marry you and leave Gudrun," said Sigurd, and his breast so heaved that the links of his hauberk snapped.' Compare this with Morris's rendering of the same passage (*Works*, VII 362): '"Rather than thou die, I will wed thee, and put away Gudrun," said Sigurd. But therewithal so swelled the heart betwixt the sides of him, that the rings of his byrny burst asunder.' Is the version by the modern scholar self-evidently better in either tone or accuracy of meaning? Morris has in fact managed to retain more of the Icelandic wording; also the climactic rhythm of the final clause and its onomatopoeic alliteration are rather fine, whilst the rendering of *en* as 'but', rather than Finch's 'and', captures more fully the dramatic irony of Sigurðr's emotions, since he actually loves Guðrún to some extent, and thus it makes better sense of Brynhildr's immediate response, which is to dismiss Sigurðr in anger.

The second objection to Morris's language, concerning the obstacles it places in the way of easy comprehension, is more damaging, however, for it is true that Morris is often likely to confuse a reader who is not already immersed in medieval literature. Again a single example must suffice here: in the interpolated poem which shows Guðrún lamenting over the body of Sigurðr, Morris makes Brynhildr curse the woman 'Who gained greeting / For thee, O Gudrun' (*Works*, VII 372). Here the word 'greeting' (= 'weeping') translates the Old Norse *grátr* (*Guðrúnarqviða in fyrsta*, 23), so Morris has adopted an archaic word, which now survives only in Scots and northern dialects,[6] for the sake of alliteration and of using a term etymologically related to the original; but he has done so at the cost of possibly being misunderstood. It must be conceded, nevertheless, that in other contexts Morris's interest in etymology and his love of recovering uncommon usages may result in creative and illuminating amplifications of the text, for example when he makes Brynhildr, speaking to Sigurðr in their final interview, say, 'I might not see clearly, or divide the good from the evil' (*Works*, VII 360), rendering *fekk ek þó eigi víst skilit* (Finch 1965, 55). Eiríkr's additional endnote (*Works*, VII 484) says that the phrase 'or divide the good from the evil' is not in the original; this is correct, but Morris's amplification is one appropriate to Brynhildr's state of mind in the context and it is prompted by the fact that the basic meaning of the verb *skilja* (here 'to discern') is 'to divide, separate'. By introducing the idea with this justification, furthermore, Morris has managed to touch on a theme that would be of major significance in his re-working of the story in his *Sigurd* poem, as discussed below.

The Story of Sigurd the Volsung and the Fall of the Niblungs (*Works* XII) was begun in October 1875 and appeared in November 1876, though the book is dated 1877.[7] For several years after publishing the *Vǫlsunga saga* translation Morris had hesitated over the attempt to make a new poem out of the saga material, in part because he thought 'no verse could render the best parts of it, and would only be a flatter and tamer version of a thing already existing', as he said in the letter to C. E. Norton mentioned above (quoted by Paul Thompson 1977, 200). There is little that is flat or tame about the *Sigurd* poem as he eventually wrote it, however. Wisely, he chose not to compete with the saga on its own terms but to give the story an essentially novelistic treatment, especially in the middle two books of the four, filling out the thoughts and emotions of the characters and floating the narrative on a stream of incidental details. For the verse he adopted a line already used in 'Iceland First Seen', a predominantly anapaestic hexameter with its caesura falling

---

[6] *OED sub* greeting, *vbl. n.*[2]

[7] From this point on, names of characters will be spelled as they appear in the poem.

almost always after the third foot, which is frequently followed by an extra syllable. It is an incantatory measure, heavily accented but variable enough when read intelligently as if out loud, and capable of sustaining long sweeps of narrative or description. Particularly impressive among the many evocative descriptions are the opening sequence, which brings the dwelling of King Volsung before the reader's eyes (*Works*, XII 1–2) and the ascent of Sigurd to the Glittering Heath (102–08) through a landscape reminiscent of Iceland, which Morris had seen for himself in 1871 and again in 1873. The line is well adapted, also, to be the vehicle for elevated set-piece speeches such as Signy's prophecy of *ragnarǫk* and the renewal of the world (22–23) or Regin's power-crazed rant when he pictures himself as possessor of the magic gold (88–89). If the poetry does flatten out and grow tame anywhere it is in the love scenes between Sigurd and Brynhild (147–48) or Sigurd and Gudrun (180–81), which are decidedly Victorian; but the scene of casual sex between Sigmund and his sister (29), in contrast, is thoroughly impressive though by no means sensationalist.

On the whole the story shadows that of the saga and the corresponding poems of the *Edda*, but some changes have been made for the sake of consistent characterization and sustained drama. In the fourth book, for example, Gudrun vindictively encourages her second spouse, Atli, to take action against her brothers for the slaying of her first husband, Sigurd, as she does in *Das Nibelungenlied* but not in the Icelandic tradition. Thus Morris completes his picture of a woman who is led by emotion, whose loving but dangerous nature is indicated by her jealousy, soon after she has met Sigurd and before she knows anything of his relationship with Brynhild, when she perceives that he longs for someone else 'and her heart grows cold as a sword' (163), and concerning whose passionate nature the narrator, putting the thought into Sigurd's mind, says, 'From the heart of a loving woman shall the death of men arise' (205). Other changes seem to have been made so as to preserve the heroic dignity of the characters; hence Morris emphasizes Sigmund's lupine nature in the account of the fight with the she-wolf (21) and makes it clear that Sigmund fought with his teeth while his hands were still fast in the stocks, but he omits the saga's comic grotesquery concerning the fact that Sigmund bit the tongue of the wolf while she was licking honey off his face. Though willing to relate the incestuous union of Sigmund and Signy, furthermore, he preserves some of the Victorian proprieties concerning cruelty to children: Gudrun does not kill the sons she has had with Atli, as she does in the saga; nor is there any mention of Sigurd's infant son, whom the saga says was killed at Brynhild's instigation and who shared their funeral pyre; and the Sigmund of the poem, unlike the same figure in the saga, does not kill the son (singular) of Signy and Siggeir when the boy fails the test of the flour bag, but sends him home to his parents (25–26). In making the last-mentioned change, it should be noted, Morris not only gives Sigmund a more sympathetic nature but also brings his behaviour into line with that revealed by his later refusal, in the poem (36) as in the saga, to kill the children who discover his hiding-place in King Siggeir's hall—though in this case the outrage is then committed by the wild and grim Sinfiotli.

As in the Old Norse sources, the gods play a role that is by no means morally unambiguous or benevolent. The appropriate attitude to be shown towards them is outlined by Brynhild in the advice she gives Sigurd at their first meeting (127):

> Love thou the Gods—and withstand them, lest thy fame should fail in the end,
> And thou be but their thrall and their bondsman, who wert born for their very friend.

By implying that the gods can be tyrannical, Brynhild partly agrees with their enemy Regin, who tells Sigurd that Loki 'gathered his godhead together' in order to kill Otter because he recognized in him 'a king of the free and the careless' (77). Sigurd, however, gives his allegiance to the gods as their friend in accordance with Brynhild's words: when he meets Odin, Sigurd declares that he will slay Fafnir for the god's sake, and adds, 'I love thee, friend of my fathers, Wise Heart of the holy folk' (109); and he addresses Regin as 'Foe of the Gods' moments before cutting off his head (117). In striking the blows against Regin and Fafnir, Sigurd is performing acts that the gods themselves cannot, for apart from their one ill-judged adventure concerning the kindred of Otter, they exhibit a strange passivity. The value of their friendship, furthermore, is to be doubted. As the dying Fafnir says with the percipience of the fey (111):

> I have seen the Gods of heaven, and their Norns withal I know:
> They love and withhold their helping, they hate and refrain the blow;
> They curse and they may not sunder, they bless and they shall not blend;
> They have fashioned the good and the evil; they abide the change and the end.

The gods, in fact, function chiefly as an audience within the narrative itself (and thus exemplify the concept of the world as story, discussed below). This can be seen best in the passage that describes the moment when Sigurd, now married to Gudrun, sees Brynhild enter the Niblung hall for the first time, recognizes her as the power of Grimhild's magic potion passes off, and understands that he must carry the burden of his knowledge 'till the last of the uttermost end' (200–01):

> The Gods look down from heaven, and the lonely King they see,
> And sorrow over his sorrow, and rejoice in his majesty.
> For the will of the Norns is accomplished, and outworn is Grimhild's spell,
> And nought now shall blind or help him, and the tale shall be to tell.

In many ways Sigurd is presented as a conventional hero of a type likely to appeal to an ethically-minded Victorian readership. He is the golden boy (102, 160), in fact a nineteenth-century solar hero (Hodgson 1999, 78), as is shown especially by his transfiguration before the dragon slaying, when Regin turns from the newly risen sun and beholds Sigurd as 'another light' (106). He is one to whom guile is alien (101) and who is troubled, after tasting the dragon's blood, when he perceives the guile and malice of the world (115). At his birth, furthermore, it is recognized that 'the best was sprung from the best' (63) and he becomes his people's hope and joy (65–67); later the Niblungs, whom he has joined, celebrate him as a bringer of law and order, of peace, freedom, and prosperity (161):

> Yea, they sing the song of Sigurd and the face without a foe,
> And they sing of the prison's rending and the tyrant laid alow, [. . .]
> And they tell how the ships of the merchants come free and go at their will,
> And how wives in peace and safety may crop the vine-clad hill.

Even when his sorrow has fallen on him and he finds himself having to share the Niblung hall with Brynhild and her husband, he is all the more 'the helper, the overcomer, the righteous sundering sword' and 'the eye-bright seer of all things, that wasteth every wrong'; and although he has become a kind of moral enforcer he remains 'the loveliest King of the King-folk'—'and all children loved him well' (205–06).

It is clear, nevertheless, that Sigurd, though an almost messianic figure, is only a 'straightener of the crooked' (206) in piecemeal fashion. The world as seen by Morris, in this period when he was becoming actively involved in politics (he became treasurer of the liberal Eastern Question Association in November 1876) but was still several years away from his adoption of Marxism (he joined the Democratic Federation in January 1883), is not capable of total and permanent transformation for the better through human means. Such a transformation belongs to the mythological *ragnarǫk* which no power can either delay or hasten, for even the gods, having made the good and the evil as Fafnir says (111, quoted above), wait for the change and the end. In this poem, in fact, Morris repudiates those who wish to bring about the wholesale reformation of life and its conditions, for he portrays them as self-glorifying and self-deceiving. Hence Grimhild, who 'deemed her life was great, / And her hand a wonder of wonders' (166), imagines that her potions will enable her to do better than the gods (166):

> For she thought: I will heal the smitten, I will raise up the smitten and slain,
> And take heed where the Gods were heedless, and build on where they began,
> And frame hope for the unborn children and the coming days of man.

In reality, however, all she does is create 'the eyeless tangle' (222) that enmeshes Sigurd and her own royal kin. Similarly and more chillingly, Regin imagines that if he can once obtain the accursed gold, on which his brother Fafnir is lying in dragon form, he will become the unique god who will have absolute control of a grateful world. Nothing at all would be done, he thinks, 'but the deed that my heart would fashion' (89):

> And there shall be no more dying, and the sea shall be as the land,
> And the world for ever and ever shall be young beneath my hand.

Against this vision of a totalitarian paradise, Sigurd, Regin's slayer, chooses the gods and the extant world with all its violence, its potential for peace and plenty, its good and its evil. He says to Regin, who fears that death may come upon him before the gold has been obtained (106):

> It is me, it is me that thou fearest, if indeed I know thy thought;
> Yes me, who would utterly light the face of all good and ill,
> If not with the fruitful beams that the summer shall fulfill,
> Then at least with the world a-blazing, and the glare of the grinded sword.

Contrasted with Sigurd, the warrior who illuminates good and ill in battle, is his killer, Guttorm, who returns from seafaring 'and is waxen fierce and strong, / A man in the wars delighting, blind-eyed through right and wrong' (202). The ability to perceive good and ill, and to distinguish them, is crucial: it is what Sigurd temporarily loses in 'the eyeless tangle', and even when his memory returns and he can see all things clearly, the situation left behind by Grimhild's plot, as Sigurd understands it, is such that 'seared is the sight of the wise, / And good is at one with evil till the new-born death shall arise' (205)—the death in question being that of Sigurd himself, and of Brynhild who brings it about. It is with reference to the same situation in the *Vǫlsunga saga* translation, in fact, that Morris had made Brynhild say that she could not see clearly 'or divide the good from the evil' (*Works*, VII 360), as discussed above. Making good and evil indistinguishable, furthermore, is presented in the *Sigurd* poem as the worst of actions, for it is not only Grimhild's crime but also the thing to which Fafnir and Regin aspired, as shown by the fact that Sigurd, having destroyed them, characterizes them in death not as evildoers but as those who 'would blend the good and the ill' (*Works*, XII 117). As to his own destruction, it is not clear whether Sigurd looks ahead to it merely as the result of the situation in which good is at one with evil, or also as a possible remedy for it; but when the moment of death comes, he certainly looks back on his life (and forward to the telling of it as a tale) and sees it as it is. 'I have done and I may not undo,' he says, but 'nought now is left to repent of, and the tale abides to tell' (230).

Sigurd's thoughts concerning the eventual tale do not simply represent the heroic wish for fame at whatever cost, as perhaps Hogni's do when he says that he will ride the steed of the Norns 'till he see great marvels and wonders, and leave great tales to be told' (203); rather they echo and answer the words spoken by Fafnir as he prepares to transform himself into a dragon and do nothing other than lie on the accursed hoard (86):

> Lo, I am a King for ever, and alone on the Gold shall I dwell
> And do no deed to repent of and leave no tale to tell.

It is a neat irony that in taking this course of action Fafnir fulfils the injunction mockingly laid by his father, Reidmar, on Odin (80):

> Then curse the world, and depart, and sit in your changeless mirth;
> And there shall be no more kings, and battle and murder shall fail,
> And the world shall laugh and long not, nor weep, nor fashion the tale.

Against the backdrop of these speeches it is clear that to Sigurd, the friend of the gods, as opposed to Fafnir and Reidmar, their enemies, it is better that there should be a tale than that the world should be free of weeping, battle or murder—even murder of himself. One of the morals of this, it would seem, is that passivity is not an option, except possibly for the gods in their role as audience (and hence for us in our role as readers), even though action will implicate the actor in guilt and involve him or her in pain; another is that a part of acting in the world must be the transformation of actions into narrative. This much is clear and certain, but we may be able to go further, albeit cautiously, since Morris makes one notable foray into the realm of the eschatological.[8] Early in the poem he makes Signy steel her brother Sigmund to face the years of

---

[8] Eschatology, the study of 'the last things', may be characterized as an attempt to describe the world as it ought to be but has not yet become. Eschatological thinking is predominantly religious but has clear relevance to some political systems such as Marxism.

strife and hardship ahead by picturing him at *ragnarǫk*; as the fight begins, she says, he will review the history known to him, and though he will have a clearer understanding of why things happen as they do, this will not change the categories of good and ill, which will remain distinct to his perception (22):

> There as thou drawest thy sword, thou shalt think of the days that were,
> And the foul shall still seem foul, and the fair shall still seem fair.

Even after the transfiguration of the world, when the last battle has ended and Baldur has returned, the memories of this life, as it now is, will remain clear and be transformed into story (22–23):

> By the side of the sons of Odin shalt thou fashion a tale to be told
> In the hall of the happy Baldur: nor there shall the tale grow old
> Of the days before the changing, e'en those that over us pass.

To put this in other words, Signy imagines that the essential nature of the world as it ought to be in its refashioned state will be one that preserves the essence of the present world by transforming it into narrative, and in which this narrative transformation has become the sole remaining act. The passage needs to be treated circumspectly because it is a piece of rhetoric put into the mouth of a peculiarly grim woman and elaborates some elements of a mythology in which Morris, of course, did not believe; nevertheless it is in no way at odds with the rest of the poem, and it serves to show us how the theme of the perception of good and ill might be combined with that of the transformation of events into narrative, and how the two might then be taken to their logical, or at least their eschatological, conclusion. If we take this aspect of the passage seriously, we find Morris putting forward, on his own terms, the Aesthetes' idea that the world exists for art, and perhaps anticipating the modern idea that its essential nature is that of a linguistic construct—the world as narrative. On the ethical and political levels, finally, it may be seen that the eschatological vision of the poem has little in common with the Marxists' end of history, to which Morris would subsequently give his allegiance, and even less with the Christians' New Jerusalem, which is more like Regin's dream of a place where all thoughts are happy, grateful, and centred on an absolute monarch; instead it is akin to what Nietzsche would later call a yea-saying, in this case one in which the world, with all its good and ill, its foul and fair, is perceived and affirmed in a narrative that is forever repeated and renewed.

In the remaining twenty years of his life, Morris changed his politics and shifted the focus of his literary output to prose, in which he produced, among other important works, the romances that initiated the genre now known as fantasy, but he never repudiated *Sigurd* or ceased to regard it as the book 'he held most highly and wished to be remembered by', according to his daughter May (*Works*, XII xxiii). Many admirers of Morris have agreed with the poet's own valuation of *Sigurd*, and no doubt there are many reasons for this, but there are two that make the judgement especially appropriate. The first is that *Sigurd*, in execution, is the most accomplished essay in refashioning by a man for whom the refashioning of existent tales was the chief mode of his poetic creativity, and who gave the idea of narrative transformation so prominent a place in his writings—above all in this poem itself. The second reason is that the Old Norse material that Morris was here seeking to make new is the story that he judged to be 'the best tale pity ever wrought' and in fact 'the grandest tale that was ever told', irrespective of language or culture. In addition there is the fact that for Morris, who came to regard Old Norse-Icelandic culture so highly and who put so much effort into making its literature available in English, the story of the Volsungs was the quintessential product of that culture, the one that appeared when 'the very heart of the North bloomed into song'. As to whether *Sigurd* is likely to be the literary work for which Morris will chiefly be remembered, this is more doubtful because some of his political pieces and romances are strong contenders in an age with little interest in narrative verse. Anyone with an interest in Old Norse, however, really ought to take a good look at this poem. The saga translations have grown old—indeed one could say that they were born old—although several, including that of *Vǫlsunga saga*, have acquired a new lease of life on the internet; but *Sigurd*, with its length and complex nature, has the quality of all great poems: although the printed text is fixed, the telling is made new every time it is read.

Bibliography

Árni Björnsson 2003. *Wagner and the Volsungs: Icelandic Sources of Der Ring des Nibelungen*.
Dentith, Simon 1999. '*Sigurd the Volsung*: Heroic Poetry in an Unheroic Age'. In Faulkner and Preston 1999, 60–70.
Faulkner, Peter 1973. *William Morris: The Critical Heritage*.
Faulkner, Peter 1980. *Against the Age: An Introduction to William Morris*.
Faulkner, Peter and Peter Preston, eds, 1999. *William Morris: Centenary Essays*.
Finch, R. G., ed. and trans., 1965. *Vǫlsunga saga: The Saga of the Volsungs*.
Hodgson, Amanda 1987. *The Romances of William Morris*.
Hodgson, Amanda 1999. 'The Troy Connection: Myth and History in *Sigurd the Volsung*'. In Faulkner and Preston 1999, 71–79.

MacCarthy, Fiona 1994. *William Morris: A Life for our Time.*
Marshall, Roderick 1979. *William Morris and his Earthly Paradises.*
Morris, William 1910–15. *The Collected Works of William Morris.* Ed. May Morris. 24 vols.
Neckel, Gustav and Hans Kuhn, eds, 1983. *Edda. Die Lieder des Codex Regius.* 5th edn.
Oberg, Charlotte H. 1978. *A Pagan Prophet: William Morris.*
OED = Oxford English Dictionary Online <http://dictionary.oed.com>
Thompson, E. P. 1977. *William Morris: Romantic to Revolutionary.*
Thompson, Paul 1977. *The Work of William Morris.*
Thorpe, Benjamin 1851–52. *Northern Mythology.* 3 vols.

IN SEARCH OF THE LAKELAND SAGA: ANTIQUARIAN FICTION AND THE NORSE SETTLEMENT IN CUMBRIA

MATTHEW TOWNEND

Few books in the nineteenth century sold more copies, or made more of a splash, than Mrs Humphry Ward's 1888 novel *Robert Elsmere*, the foremost example of the so-called genre of 'cassock-ripper' (Gilmour 1993, 89), in which a young clergyman painfully loses his faith. In the third chapter of *Robert Elsmere*, the eponymous hero is to be found making dinner-table conversation at a house in the fictional valley of Long Whindale, based upon the Westmorland valley of Longsleddale (Lindop 1993, 30). A social solecism by the mercurial Dr Baker leads to abrupt silence and conversational paralysis, at which juncture the young hero demonstrates the stuff of which he is made (1888, 65):

> Robert Elsmere alone showed presence of mind. Bending across to Dr. Baker, he asked him a sudden question as to the history of a certain strange green mound or barrow that rose out of a flat field not far from the vicarage windows. Dr. Baker grasped his whiskers, threw the young man a queer glance, and replied. Thenceforward he and Robert kept up a lively antiquarian talk on the traces of Norse settlement in the Cumbrian valleys, which lasted till the ladies left the dining-room.

From this curious episode it would seem, then, that Norse settlement in the area was a fertile and familiar subject at the dinner-tables of the Cumbrian professional classes in the 1880s, and a good way of making conversation. In late-Victorian Lakeland, in other words, the Vikings were news, and worthy of discussion, and it is one aspect of this phenomenon that I want to look at in this essay. This was not, of course, a phenomenon restricted to the Lake District: as Andrew Wawn's work has shown, in nineteenth-century Britain 'Old Northernism' took many forms and fuelled many enthusiasms (Wawn 2000). The present essay may thus be regarded as a contribution from a distinctively regional perspective to this larger subject, so many aspects of which have been brilliantly delineated and explored by Wawn.

The importance of the Norse influence on the Lake District was first argued for in a sustained manner by no less a figure than Thomas De

Quincey, in a four-part essay in the *Westmorland Gazette* in 1819 and 1820. De Quincey noted that certain words in Cumbrian dialect resembled comparable words in modern Danish, and suggested a link between the two. As D. S. Roberts has shown (1999), the influence of De Quincey's insight can be increasingly seen in the successive editions of Wordsworth's *Guide to the Lakes*—for Victorian readers, of course, the single most important publication on the region. The study of Norse influence on the area received its next major stimulus in 1856, when Robert Ferguson published his influential—if variable— monograph entitled *The Northmen in Cumberland and Westmoreland*, and from this point onwards the study of Norse antiquities in Cumbria never looked back. Burials, sculpture, inscriptions, dialect, place- names, surnames, folk-customs, furniture, buildings, sheep, wrestling: in the latter decades of the century all these and other subjects received increasing antiquarian interest—some well-founded, scholarly, and perceptive, and some not. At the turn of the century, however, two men— one a good antiquarian and the other a quite exceptional one—tried to go one step further than this, and instead of simply studying Viking antiquities in the Lake District they endeavoured to add to them themselves, by the composition of some original native saga-literature for the Lake District, modelled deliberately upon the great Family Sagas of medieval Iceland. These men were William Gershom Colling- wood and Charles Arundel Parker, and their sagas are *Thorstein of the Mere*, *The Bondwoman*, and *The Story of Shelagh, Olaf Cuaran's Daughter*.

Collingwood is of course much the more famous of the two, and will take centre-stage here, with Parker in something of a supporting role. Born in Liverpool in 1854, Collingwood studied at Oxford and the Slade School of Art, before settling down in the Lakes at Lanehead, a big house overlooking Coniston Water, where he acted as unofficial secre- tary (and, in time, biographer and editor) to the elderly John Ruskin, and threw himself whole-heartedly into the study of Lake District antiqui- ties. Collingwood's first paper on the Norse influence on the region was published in 1894 (with footnotes supplied by Eiríkr Magnússon, William Morris' Icelandic collaborator); but that this first publication was only the tip of an iceberg of prior research became clear in the following two years, with the delivery of a seminal paper to the recently- formed Viking Club in London (Collingwood 1896b), and the appearance of his two fictional works on the subject: *Thorstein of the Mere* in 1895, and *The Bondwoman* in 1896. The former was dedicated to Collingwood's young son Robin, in time to far outshine his father, as a philosopher and historian of Roman Britain.[1]

Charles Arundel Parker was just a few years older than Collingwood, having been born in Chatham in 1851. He trained as a physician at Edinburgh University, but in 1877 settled back at the family home near Gosforth, at the entrance to Wasdale, where until his death he acted as, variously, G. P., J. P., churchwarden, and general stalwart of the local community. Unlike Collingwood, his main antiquarian interests were not in origin Norse, but simply (and intensely) local, and were focussed upon the remarkable array of pre-conquest stone sculpture associated with St. Mary's Church, Gosforth (where, incidentally, for part of Parker's time the rector was John Wordsworth, grandson of the poet) (Parker 1904, 74). In 1882 Parker discovered the so-called Gosforth Fishing Stone, and in 1896, in the course of church renovations, he was instrumental in the discovery of the Gosforth hogbacks: these monuments, and the more famous free-standing cross in the churchyard, he described and analysed in a sequence of increasingly astute publications: a brief pamphlet in 1882 (complete with a sonnet by Canon Rawnsley, friend of Beatrix Potter and co-founder of the National Trust), a lengthier monograph in 1896, and a thorough guide-book in 1904. Finally, in 1909 he published a fictional account of the origins of these monuments: *The Story of Shelagh, Olaf Cuaran's Daughter*.[2]

Here, then, we have two antiquarian writers to consider, who, it should be said, knew each other well and were friends, and even collaborated on some publications: their co-authored 1917 article on the Gosforth Cross remains foundational, and is also the main source for the guide-book still being sold at Gosforth Church. Here we have two writers who respond to the importance of Norse antiquities in their beloved

---

[1] On W. G. Collingwood's antiquarianism and his influences on R. G. Collingwood see Johnson 1994 and Parker 2001. For biographical accounts see the *Oxford Dictionary of National Biography* and contemporary obituaries in *The Times* (3rd October 1932) and the *Transactions of the Cumberland and Westmorland Antiquarian and Archaeological Society* (New Series 33 (1932–33), 308–12). More intimate portraits are offered by his grand-daughter (Altounyan 1969, 1990) and Arthur Ransome (1976, 91–97). On Collingwood's Norse enthusiasms see Wawn 1992, 223–28, and 2000, 335–40.

[2] For Parker's biography see his obituary in the *Transactions of the Cumberland and Westmorland Antiquarian and Archaeological Society* (New Series 18 (1918), 243–45).

region of the country by writing fictional accounts of the activities of Viking settlers in the Lake District in the ninth and tenth centuries. These fictional accounts in many ways stand in a clear relation to the sagas of medieval Iceland, and my argument is that in some sense Collingwood and Parker are endeavouring to supply a native equivalent to these famous medieval works—they are attempting to provide a saga-literature for the English Lake District. In what follows, therefore, there are three questions I want to address. First, why did these writers want to attempt such a thing? Second (and most fully), how did they go about doing so? And third (and in conclusion), how well did they succeed?

First, then, why, and the simple answer is that the nineteenth-century antiquarians came to see Iceland and Lakeland as parallel colonies and parallel cultures, both being settlements made by migrating Scandinavians during the Viking Age. Indeed, in some respects one may say that Victorian scholars perceived this truth—that Iceland and Lakeland were parallel and equal Viking colonies—rather more clearly than contemporary ones: it is important not to think that in some sense Iceland is primary and Lakeland secondary simply because Iceland was the one Scandinavian colony that persisted into the post-medieval period in recognizably Scandinavian form. At the time of Viking-Age expansion Iceland was no more (or no less) part of the Scandinavian world than Lakeland: and the recognition of this led the way in the later nineteenth century to a fuller exploration of the linguistic, cultural, and historical parallels between Lakeland and Iceland—for instance in lengthily-titled monographs in 1894 and 1895 by the Reverend Thomas Ellwood, rector of Torver near Coniston, and an enthusiastic if under-informed student of Norse language and culture (see further Wawn 1995 and 2000, 228–30). But in one obvious and important respect these two Norse colonies were different: in literary terms, the settlement in Iceland had resulted in the immense achievement of the medieval sagas; but the settlement in Lakeland was silent and unrecorded, and it was this silence, this gap in the cultural remains, that Collingwood and Parker were endeavouring to rectify with their provision of Lakeland sagas. As Collingwood observes in the introductory pages to his 1902 guide-book *The Lake Counties* (1902, 4):

> Story alone and scenery alone may interest specialists, but the thing that appeals to us all, and charms us, and carries us out of ourselves, is the union of story and scenery. Then you get poetry and romance.

Manifesto statements by both writers make it quite clear that this provision of Lakeland sagas was indeed their purpose, and both are worth quoting at some length. Collingwood writes as follows in his postscript to *Thorstein*, entitled 'Remarks on the Norse Settlement' (1895, 307–08):

> Our antiquaries, however, have found us no Lakeland Saga. The reason is simple. By the time when the Sagas were written down, the Norman Conquest and the feudal organisation of England had cut these Norse colonists away from their kindred [...]. Whatever songs and stories of Viking ancestors were then current in the mouths of the people found no scribe such as Ari the learned, or Hall Gizurson. One would have thought that in the abbeys of the district some native monk might have noted them down, as the Icelandic folklore was noted down at Flatey, and Helgafell. But the great abbeys hereabouts were founded by aliens, and their mental life had no room for local patriotism. [...] The saga-period went by; and in another couple of centuries, when the age of Border ballads had set in, there were new themes in plenty to sing about. The old legends were out of mind, except for isolated traditions and surviving names.
>
> And yet, even at this day, enough of these remain to give us glimpses of the past. [...] And so to write this story of Thorstein of the Mere—the *eponymus* of our Thurston-water (Coniston Lake)—is only as it were to string afresh a handful of broken beads from an opened cairn. There was a Thorstein's saga, no doubt, once upon a time; or at least ballads of the giants on the fell, and the invasion of Eadmund. 'Thus sung, or would, or could, or should have sung' the local skald.

Parker, evidently drawing on Collingwood's earlier formulation, confirms this view in his 'Fore Word' to *The Story of Shelagh* (1909, v–vi):

> The reason why no Lake Country saga has survived is not far to seek. The only person who had sufficient culture and leisure to write one out would be a monk, who was not above associating with the people; and the monks were either Norman or leaned to the Norman party then in power, who regarded all Englishmen as barbarians; and not only made little distinction between Norse, Angle, and Welsh, but knew little and cared less for their history and belief.
>
> Yet there must have been many a saga tale told round the fire on winter evenings in the homesteads of Cumberland. Not only those of old Norway, but of heroes and deeds belonging to the Lake Country; while women spun, men made nets, carved woodwork and mended gear, and children listened with round eyes until bidden away to bed. Such a tale might mayhap take the form of this story.

The conditional tenses with which Parker and Collingwood con-clude their reflections ('might mayhap', and the Byronic 'would, or could, or should have') act as invitations to fill the silence, rather than deterrents.

An alternative approach to the question 'why' would be in terms of regional fiction. As Keith Snell has shown (1998), there was an upsurge in interest in regional fiction—its writing and its reading—all over the country from the mid-1880s onwards, an upsurge clearly related to concurrent interests in, for example, local dialects and local antiquities. Among the great Victorian novelists, one need only think of Thomas Hardy to perceive the force of this movement. Regional fiction often means regional publication and regional readership, and it is no coincidence that Parker's *Story of Shelagh* (like many of Collingwood's other works, including the 1909 reprint of *Thorstein*) was published by Titus Wilson of Kendal (until 1990 the printer of *Saga-Book*, the periodical of the Viking Society for Northern Research). As Snell comments (1998, 42),

> the regional novel in many of its forms provides a focus for the study of readers' expectations about the locality and region *vis-à-vis* a wider area such as the nation state, and for the study of those elements (e.g. speech, dialect, social relations, topography, local tradition) that form the basis for local consciousness and a sense of attachment.

In other words, regional fiction supplies a space in which issues of regional identity—often defined historically—can be thought through and articulated.

So much, therefore, for the question, why write a Lakeland saga: there was a parallelism between Iceland and Lakeland, but also a silence on the Lakeland side that needed to be filled; and such an intention fits cogently into broader issues of regional identity in the late nineteenth century. And there is no doubt at all that the works to fill it were to be sagas, and not novels, or tales, or stories. Indeed, one can see in the subtitles of these works a hardening of the conception and a proclamation of them as substitute sagas: *Thorstein* is labelled as a 'saga' from the very beginning (and at an early stage Collingwood toyed with the idea of calling it *Fornesinga saga*, or the saga of the people of Furness), but *The Bondwoman*'s original status as a 'story' is altered in its later revision to a 'saga' (indeed, to 'a saga of Langdale', like *Fornesinga saga* forming an obvious parallel to geographically-titled Icelandic sagas such as *Laxdœla saga* and *Ljósvetninga saga*). As for Parker, Titus Wilson's publicity flier advertised the forthcoming *Story of Shelagh* as a 'saga tale' (Figure 1), but it had simply become a 'saga' by the time the title-page was printed. In his postscript to *Thorstein* Collingwood playfully characterizes himself as a 'belated Sagaman', and this self-presentation informs much of what he is attempting in his two works. In scrutinizing

Figure 1: Advertisement for C.A. Parker, *The Story of Shelagh, Olaf Cuaran's Daughter* (Kendal: Titus Wilson, 1909)

Figure 2: Title-page for W.G. Collingwood, *Thorstein of the Mere: A Saga of the Northmen in Lakeland* (London: Edward Arnold, 1895)

the illustrated title-page to the first edition of *Thorstein*, drawn by Collingwood himself, sharp-eyed runologists will note that the decorated panel at the top contains the simple inscription in Norse runes *Þorsteins saga* (Figure 2).

Secondly, how did these two writers go about the composition of their Lakeland sagas? In antiquarian works such as these, it is more than usually difficult to distinguish the elements that go into their making from those that go into their meaning, as so many of the historical details function as both source and allusion at one and the same time. Essentially, though, two obvious bodies of material condition the ways in which Collingwood and Parker construct their narratives: Norse Lakeland antiquities, and medieval Icelandic sagas, and this twofold origin is apparent in terms of both substance and form. So, for instance, *The Bondwoman* contains within its brief space such standard saga-episodes and motifs as horse-fights, fostering, concubinage, the exposure of infants, haymaking, prophecy, and the feasts of *vetr-nætr* and *Jólablót*. As for material culture, Collingwood observes in his endnotes to *Thorstein* that 'It may be said here that the dress, manners, &c., of the story are based on sagas or archaeological evidence, compared with Lake District characteristics' (1895, 319): examples of this occur in the forms of wood-carving, ironwork, bloomeries, weaponry, thing-mounts, head-wear, and house-remains. For Parker, the most important objects of material culture are the stone monuments of Gosforth. In *The Story of Shelagh* he offers aetiological accounts of how each of these came into being: the Fishing Stone is presented as the funeral cross of Shelagh's husband Vikar, one of the hogbacks is Shelagh's grave-marker and the other that of her son Griss, and the great Gosforth Cross itself is a memorial stone to Shelagh, used as a preaching-cross and exemplifying her role in the conversion of the Gosforth settlers from paganism to Christianity.

The methodology here is plain enough. Tom Shippey, in his influential work on Tolkien, has written persuasively of the nineteenth-century philological belief in what he terms 'asterisk-reality' (1982, 15–18); that is, the reconstruction of older states of the language which are not recorded in any extant documents, and hence are prefaced by an asterisk, but which can be recaptured through a scientific and dependable methodology. What Collingwood and Parker are attempting in their Lakeland sagas is a form of what one might term 'asterisk-history'— observing later forms and evidence, and from these reconstructing an earlier state with a comparable belief in the accuracy, broadly speaking, of the reconstructive method.

This attempt at asterisk-history can be seen especially clearly when one considers these works as tales of origins and settlement. Chronologically, the early history of Iceland is often separated into the so-called Age of Settlement (from 870 to 930) and the so-called Saga Age (from 930 to 1030), and this chronology is closely followed by Collingwood and Parker—naturally so, since Iceland and Lakeland can be seen as parallel settlements. In *Thorstein of the Mere* Thorstein's father Swein settles at Greenodd at the foot of the Crake valley in 913, and the eponymous outlaw-hero is finally killed in 945. *The Bondwoman* covers a much briefer space of time, as befits its more local narrative, and is restricted to the years 970 and 971, right at the heart of the Saga Age; while *The Story of Shelagh* begins with the settlement of Scandinavians in the Gosforth district between 890 and 905, and concludes with the death of Shelagh's son Griss in 1020. These dates are given in the chronological tables which both Collingwood and Parker supply as appendices, and, as well as corresponding to Icelandic saga-chronology, they are carefully correlated with the few appearances of the region in the *Anglo-Saxon Chronicle*: namely the successive harryings of Cumberland or Westmorland by King Edmund in 945, Earl Thored in 966, and King Æthelred in the year 1000, all three of which appear in the narrative of one or other of these Lakeland sagas, as do other events recorded in early medieval sources.

In terms of origins and settlement, an important principle is that many of the dramatis personae, and some of the plot, of these narratives are derived from place-name evidence. The search for the Lakeland saga arguably began to take concrete shape in 1893, when Collingwood began to plot Norse settlement-names on a map of the Lake District, an exercise that kick-started his local medieval interests as never before. Maps remain an essential part of these three works in their published form (just as ever since Morris and Magnússon no modern edition or translation of an Icelandic saga is complete without a map of the area of action—and Collingwood and Jón Stefánsson's 1902 translation of *Kormaks saga* is no exception). On the maps in these works (Figure 3), both writers endeavour to plot Norse place-names in their postulated Old Norse form, though of the two, Collingwood is by far the better philologist (indeed, it is clear that Parker's knowledge of Old Norse is fairly rudimentary); and a similar Collingwood-influenced map occurs in Henry Swainson Cowper's 1899 history of the parish of Hawkshead.

An important appendix to *Thorstein*, earlier scrutinized by Eiríkr Magnússon in draft form, carefully lists Lake District place-names with

In Search of the Lakeland Saga

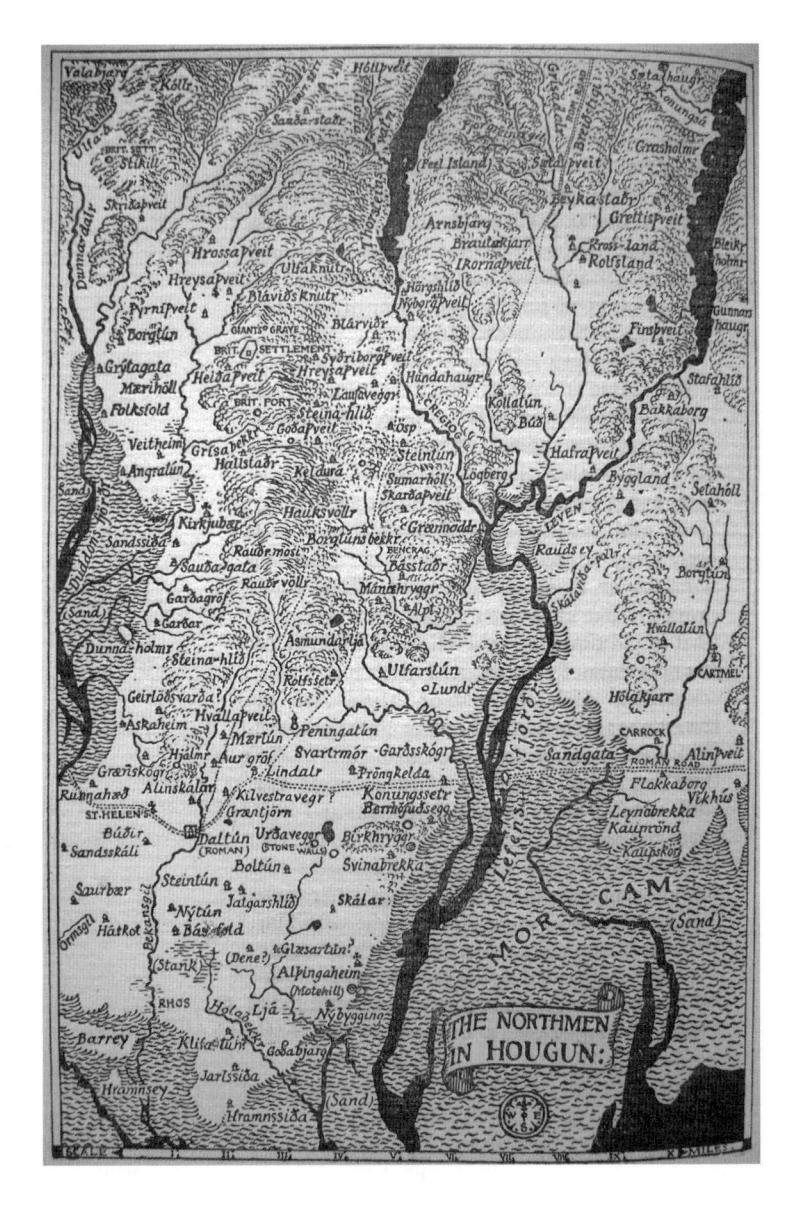

Figure 3: Map of the Norse settlements in Furness, in W.G. Collingwood, *Thorstein of the Mere: A Saga of the Northmen in Lakeland* (London: Edward Arnold, 1895), p. 32

modern, medieval, and postulated Old Norse forms—showing an appreciation of the methodology of place-name study of the kind mostly lacking in the work of Ferguson and Ellwood, and aptly demonstrating why the great Swedish scholar Eilert Ekwall, a good friend, reckoned Collingwood a shrewd toponymist (Ekwall 1922, vii). Collingwood and Parker harness the energy of etymologies to supply events: for instance, the narrative climax of *The Bondwoman* reconstructs the encounter behind the place-name Orrest near Windermere (from Old Norse *orrosta*, meaning 'battle'), and from the very first Collingwood planned *Thorstein* as a place-name-derived narrative.

Above all, Collingwood and Parker use place-names to recover a cast of Norse actors: a form, one might even say, of 'asterisk-biography'. In *Thorstein* Collingwood unlocks the etymologies of Norse settlement-names in the area around Greenodd and Ulverston to recover a population of settlers, the original Lakeland *landnámsmenn* who took land along the coastal regions before their descendants—figures like Thorstein himself—later ventured inland to occupy the valleys (1895, 34–35; identifications in square brackets are added):

> Beside Ulfar there settled others of the Northmen along the coast. There would have been Raven at the south point of Foreness, from whom we call Rampside and Ramsey. Beyond Barr-ey, that is Barley island there is Orm's Gill, and round about it the villages into which his folk spread; Hawcott, the high cottage; Sowerby, the muddy farm; Sandscale, the shed by the sand; and so forth. [. . .] After a while, from these first settlements on the coast, land was taken up inbank by the families and followers of the first viking settlers. Around Ulfar's town [Ulverston] there were Rolf's seat [Rosset], and Asmund's lea [Osmotherley], and Hauk's vale [Hawkswell], and Máni's riggs [Mansriggs].

Parker later employs the same technique, at one point in his narrative cataloguing the various settlers who come together at the Thing or assembly place at Gallabanks near Gosforth (1909, 45):

> Now there came to Gillibanc [Gallabanks] on the third morn after the sending of the bodes, Rognvald Ormson, whose fore-elder was Avelin of the glas [Ravenglass], Viberg Vibergson from the thwaite by Esk [Waberthwaite], and Korni from the fell [Corney], with their neighbour Siward from Langlifergh [Langley], the last in a great way about his young wife Langlif. To them came Hamal from the head of the great mere [Ambleside], Hallbiorn from his oatfields on the Mealholm [Holborn Hill, Millom], Ailward from Borgartun [Broughton-in-Furness], Thurstan from Konungstun [Coniston], and Arnold Ulfson from Duddon [Ulpha]. Bardi Haukson was there from his barrow in Vasdal [Wasdale]; Gudda from Guddathveit [Godderthwaite], Stefnir from Stefenergh [Stepheney]; and Hundi from his home among the

rowans men still call Reynira [Rainors]; with a host of folk from Bekkjarmot [Beckermet] and the Egen [Ehen], and from every thwaite and garth and setr of the Norsemen.

Conspicuous in both these passages is how localized these place-name-derived narratives are. Indeed, exactly how localized (and, therefore, personalized) becomes clear from the siting of Parker's Thing meeting: at Gallabanks, which, as he points out in his guide-book *The Gosforth District*, is directly opposite the old house called Parknook near Gosforth (1904, 61); what Parker does not point out, however, is that this is, in fact, his own house, the Parker family seat. The obvious parallels to these passages are the early chapters in many Family Sagas that detail the arrival and settlement in Iceland of the ancestors of the main characters, and above all the Icelandic *Landnámabók* or 'Book of Settlements' (unreliably translated by Ellwood in 1898).

Even from such a brief survey as this, one can gain some sense of how the substance of these works derives from both Lakeland antiquities and Icelandic sagas; and the same is true of the form of the books, including the style in which they are written. The Lakeland input comes from the heavy use of local dialect (as noted in Wawn 2000, 337–38), especially terms of a probable Norse derivation (as observed by De Quincey, Ferguson, Ellwood, and many others): this ranges from simple vocabulary (for instance, *stee*, *wath*, *to speer*, *to lait*, *to greet*, and so on) to the use of extended idioms and proverbs ('go thy gate', 'riving and rugging like a lad at his laiks', 'The plough gangs bain twixt rig and raine'). The Icelandic input comes from the degree to which Collingwood (as the better Norse scholar) frequently endeavours to reproduce saga-style (again, as noted in Wawn 2000, 335). This can be seen from a number of illustrative practices: for example, by the calquing of English words and phrases on Norse ones (for instance, 'land-take' for Old Norse *landnám*, 'town' for Old Norse *tún* 'home-meadow', 'hundred' for Old Norse *hundrað* '120'); it can also be seen by the saga-formulae by which the tales end ('So ends the story of Thorstein', 'And that is the end of the story', 'So ends the story of Shelagh'), and by which characters enter and leave the saga ('There was a man called Swein', 'And so Asdis goes out of the story'). For an extended example one may glance at the opening of a related tale, Collingwood's 'Story of Thurstan at the Thwaite', in which the painfulness of the Norman division of Cumbria in 1163 is explored through the *ancien régime* figure of Thorstein's great-great-great-grandson (discussed also in Wawn 2000, 335–36). The tale (which perhaps corresponds to an Icelandic *páttr* or short story) opens as follows (1899, 40–41):

Thurstan hight a man. He was Swainson: Swain was Thurstanson: and their fore-elder was Swain, the son of Thurstan of the Mere. He dwelt at the Thwaite; that is at Conyngs-tun in the land of Hougun, by the side of the mere that was his mere. He was a stout man and a strong man of his hands, but elderly, and stirred out little from his fields downbank along the waterhead and the garths on the how aback of his hall. For he saw the way things were going, and liked it not: being a man of the old sort, and not given to change.

It would take no great effort to translate this into Old Norse saga-prose: one can observe the formulaic opening (*Þorsteinn hét maðr*), the simple syntax, the emphasis when introducing a character on genealogy and a few descriptive epithets, and the resultant implication that character is relatively set or fixed. Poignantly, one can also note that the protagonist's name is now Anglicized in form, rather than Old Norse like that of his famous ancestor (Thurstan, not Thorstein): itself a linguistic marker of the erosion and loss of Norse culture and autonomy which the story explores. Such a conspicuous duplication of saga-style is by no means the only narrative style and point of view adopted by Collingwood, but it is sufficiently present to mark it out as a deliberate strategy and one of the many ways by which the status of Lakeland saga is attempted.

The third and last of my three main questions in this essay is, how well do Collingwood and Parker succeed in supplying Lakeland sagas? It is first worth noting that both writers clearly succeeded well enough to inspire later followers, in which respect Collingwood was arguably more fortunate than Parker. Parker died in 1918, and was buried in Gosforth churchyard, but *The Story of Shelagh* was thoroughly (and explicitly) recycled and rewritten by Nicholas Size, proprietor of the Victoria Family Hotel, Buttermere, in his 1932 story *Shelagh of Eskdale*—a work that can seem sadly deficient in literary and historical skills. Size's better-known book is his pseudo-history of Buttermere, *The Secret Valley*, and he also published a novel about Óláfr Tryggvason (Size 1929 and 1933). Collingwood's later follower was, however, of a different order altogether. In 1896 Collingwood received a fan-letter praising *Thorstein of the Mere* from the Professor of History at the Yorkshire College (later the University of Leeds), and the following summer Collingwood's family met up with the Professor's family for a pre-arranged picnic on Peel Island on Coniston Water. In 1903 the Professor's son pitched up in Coniston as a struggling young journalist, and had the good fortune to be befriended by the Collingwood family. The young journalist was Arthur Ransome, and from these early days until his death in 1932

Collingwood acted as a substitute father-figure to the younger man. The firstfruits of Ransome's willing adoption was his 1904 Viking story 'Rolf Sigurdson', dedicated to Collingwood's daughter Dora and later reprinted in his whimsical collection *The Hoofmarks of the Faun* (Ransome 1911); but the true, more oblique homage, as opposed to direct imitation or emulation, was to come somewhat later. As indicated by its centrality on Collingwood's title-page (Figure 2), the climax of *Thorstein of the Mere* comes when the outlawed Thorstein takes refuge on Peel Island on Coniston Water (in an episode clearly influenced by the hero's refuge on Drangey in *Grettis saga*), while in Ransome's *Swallows and Amazons* series Peel Island becomes Wild Cat Island. For those with ears to hear, there is even a veiled allusion to Thorstein's earlier outlawry in Ransome's novel: 'What a place,' muses able-seaman Titty on first landing on Wild Cat Island, 'I expect somebody hid on the island hundreds of years ago, and kept his boat here' (1938, 54). When *Thorstein* was republished by Heinemann in 1929, Ransome gave it a lively publicity puff in his regular Saturday column in the *Manchester Guardian*, while later in his posthumously-published *Autobiography*, he recalled life with the Collingwoods in glowing terms and described *Thorstein* as 'the best-loved book of my boyhood' (1976, 81): a testament to the enormous effect that this Lakeland saga was indirectly to have on twentieth-century children's literature.

In fact, Collingwood and Parker may have been more like Icelandic saga-authors than they realized. Their works date from a time when there was still a widespread belief in the detailed accuracy of the Icelandic sagas as historical documents, as well as a strong degree of belief in the so-called 'freeprose' theory of their genesis (that is, the belief that the extant sagas are basically transcribed versions of originally oral tales). But according to some later 'bookprose' thinking, of a type epitomized by Sigurður Nordal and the so-called Icelandic school, the Icelandic Family Sagas were in fact composed and created in just the same way as Collingwood and Parker's Lakeland sagas: that is, by observing later forms and reconstructing earlier states, as for example in the early chapters of Family Sagas that appear to invent figures and incidents of settlement from surviving place-names (the opening of *Laxdæla saga* would be a good example). In other words, Collingwood and Parker, and the thirteenth-century Icelandic saga-authors, might all be regarded as antiquarians engaged in historical and imaginative reconstruction, and with many of the same issues operative for both groups in terms of local identity and cultural inheritance; and this remains true in our current scholarly climate, with our renewed interest in oral sources and local traditions in the genesis of the sagas (see for example Gísli Sigurðsson 2004).

In reality, of course, these Lakeland sagas were never intended to deceive anyone. The intention, as has been seen, was to be as rigorous as possible in reconstructive methods (especially with regard to settlement-narratives), and to avoid the prodigal inventiveness of deliberate fiction. But even if there was truth in these works—even if the reconstructed sagas fitted the maps and the monuments—still there was no avoiding the fact that these were after all modern productions, and not medieval ones, and these belated sagas could never be anything other than wistful and imaginative antiquarianism. Iceland and Lakeland were perceived as parallel settlements; but they were not parallel in the heritage that survived into the post-medieval period in general, and into the 1890s in particular.

In the summer of 1897, after he had written his two Lakeland sagas (and translated, though not yet published, *Kormaks saga*), Collingwood spent three months travelling round Iceland with the native scholar Jón Stefánsson, drawing and painting the pictures that would illustrate the sumptuous account of their journey, *A Pilgrimage to the Saga-steads of Iceland* (1899). Andrew Wawn has noted how on his return home to Coniston Collingwood's letters to Eiríkr Magnússon express distress and disillusion at the state of Iceland in the 1890s; and Collingwood's letters home to his family written in the course of his travels contain similar sentiments (Collingwood 1996). Wawn suggests that one of the results of this disillusion is that 'there was a sense in which Collingwood felt that the Lake District was now more Icelandic in spirit if not in scenery than Iceland itself' (1992, 226), since it is in Lakeland that the supposed Viking virtues of thrift, energy, and initiative are now to be encountered. This may well be so in some respects (though the idea of a transfer of 'Icelandicness' implies a privileging of Iceland over Lakeland rather than an equality between the two), but in literary terms it could never be the case.

I would like to end with another, briefer product of Collingwood's 1897 pilgrimage, namely a short poem entitled 'In Gunnar's Country', which ponders the landscape around Hlíðarendi, the homestead of the famous saga-hero Gunnarr Hámundarson of *Njáls saga*. Until its 1996 reprinting in Collingwood's 'Letters from Iceland', edited by his grand-daughter, this poem had only ever been published once, in the September 1897 edition of *Nothing Much: A Monthly Magazine*—and since this was an in-house, manuscript journal compiled by Collingwood's children, one may assume that its readership was not great. Dated 'Fljótshlíð. Aug. 4. 1897.', the poem reads as follows (Collingwood 1996, 74):

> Because you bring a tale of old
> Before these eyes made visible,
> And tender words made audible
> Within these ears, O mountains cold,
> O desolate shores, O wasted wold,
> I sit content beneath your spell.
>
> Not for yourselves. Nay, take it not
> Ill said; but sweeter hues elsewhere,
> Forms fairer, lovelier lines are there
> For eye to gloat on, unforgot:
> Where crag and tarn, and glade and grot
> Stand peerless yet, beyond compare:
>
> But voiceless; like the bride of stone
> That knew no childish rogueries,
> Nor any girlish melodies,
> Nor passionate words, though woman grown.
> —Which would a man for very own?—
> The image—or the memories?

This poem has been helpfully discussed by Andrew Wawn (1997), who reads it, no doubt rightly, in the context of Collingwood's increasing homesickness. My point here is a simple one (made also by Wawn), which is that the poem expresses very clearly indeed the perceived distinctions between the two Viking colonies. Iceland preserved the words and the associations, but its harsh landscape was 'cold', 'desolate', and 'wasted'. The landscape of Lakeland, on the other hand, was not only comparatively 'sweeter', 'fairer', and 'lovelier' than Iceland, but superlatively 'peerless' and 'beyond compare'. But, as Collingwood makes plain with dexterous enjambement between stanzas, Lakeland remains 'voiceless'. It will be recalled that in *The Lake Counties* Collingwood declared that 'the thing that appeals to us all, and charms us, and carries us out of ourselves, is the union of story and scenery' (1902, 4). This poem therefore crystallizes the contrastive blessings of the two parallel colonies, and, in its closing lines, the conflict that would arise if one had to choose between them. No Lakeland saga-literature can compare with the Icelandic, and no Icelandic landscape can compare with Lakeland. The two remain contrastive, in complementary distribution: and it is perhaps only natural therefore that Lakeland antiquarians should attempt to marry the two within the format of the Lakeland saga, since otherwise one must choose, in the terms of Collingwood's own formulations, between image and memory, scenery and story.

Bibliography

Altounyan, Taqui 1969. *In Aleppo Once.*
Altounyan, Taqui 1990. *Chimes From A Wooden Bell: A Hundred Years in the Life of a Euro-Armenian Family.*
Collingwood, W. G., with notes by Eiríkr Magnússon 1894–95. 'Some Manx Names in Cumbria'. *Transactions of the Cumberland and Westmorland Antiquarian and Archaeological Society.* Old Series 13, 403–14.
Collingwood, W. G. 1895. *Thorstein of the Mere: A Saga of the Northmen in Lakeland.*
Collingwood, W. G. 1896a. *The Bondwoman: A Story of the Northmen in Lakeland.* Revised and republished as *The Bondwomen: A Saga of Langdale* (1932).
Collingwood, W. G. 1896b. 'The Vikings in Lakeland: their Place-Names, Remains, History'. *Saga-Book* 1, 182–96.
C[ollingwood], W. G. 1899. *Coniston Tales.*
Collingwood, W. G. 1902. *The Lake Counties.*
Collingwood, W. G. 1996. 'Letters from Iceland'. Ed. Janet Gnosspelius. *Collingwood Studies* 3, 1–75.
Collingwood, W. G. and Jón Stefánsson 1899. *A Pilgrimage to the Sagasteads of Iceland.*
Collingwood, W. G. and Jón Stefánsson, trans., 1902. *The Life and Death of Cormac the Skald: Being the Icelandic Kormáks Saga Rendered into English.*
Cowper, Henry Swainson 1899. *Hawkshead (the Northernmost Parish of Lancashire): Its History, Archæology, Industries, Folklore, Dialect, Etc, Etc.*
De Quincey, Thomas 1819–20. 'Danish Origin of the Lake Country Dialect'. *Westmorland Gazette* 13 November 1819, 1 December 1819, 18 December 1819, and 8 January 1820. Reprinted in *The Works of Thomas De Quincey*: Volume I, *Writings 1799–1820.* Ed. Barry Symonds 2000, 292–310.
Ekwall, Eilert 1922. *The Place-Names of Lancashire.*
Ellwood, Thomas 1894. *The Landnama Book of Iceland as it Illustrates the Dialect, Place Names, Folk Lore and Antiquities of Cumberland, Westmorland and North Lancashire.*
Ellwood, Thomas 1895. *Lakeland and Iceland: Being A Glossary of Words in the Dialect of Cumberland, Westmorland and North Lancashire which Seem Allied to or Identical with the Icelandic or Norse.*
Ellwood, Thomas, trans., 1898. *The Book of the Settlement of Iceland.*
Ferguson, Robert 1856. *The Northmen in Cumberland and Westmoreland.*
Gilmour, Robin 1993. *The Victorian Period: The Intellectual and Cultural Context of English Literature, 1830–1890.*

Gísli Sigurðsson 2004. *The Medieval Icelandic Saga and Oral Tradition: A Discourse on Method*. Trans. Nicholas Jones.

Johnson, Douglas H. 1994. 'W. G. Collingwood and the Beginnings of the Idea of History'. *Collingwood Studies* 1, 1–26.

Lindop, Grevel 1993. *A Literary Guide to the Lake District*.

Oxford Dictionary of National Biography: <http://www.oxforddnb.com/>

Parker, C. A. 1882. *The Runic Crosses at Gosforth, Cumberland*.

Parker, C. A. 1896. *The Ancient Crosses at Gosforth, Cumberland*.

Parker, C. A. 1904. *The Gosforth District: Its Antiquities and Places of Interest*.

Parker, C. A. 1909. *The Story of Shelagh, Olaf Cuaran's Daughter: A Saga of the Northmen in Cumberland in the Tenth Century*.

Parker, C. A. and W. G. Collingwood 1917. 'A Reconsideration of Gosforth Cross'. *Transactions of the Cumberland and Westmorland Antiquarian and Archaeological Society*. New Series 17, 99–113.

Parker, Christopher 2001. 'W. G. Collingwood's Lake District'. *Northern History* 38, 295–313.

Ransome, Arthur 1911. *The Hoofmarks of the Faun*.

Ransome, Arthur 1929. 'Drawn at a Venture: Thorstein's Country'. *Manchester Guardian* 30 November 1929.

Ransome, Arthur [1930] 1938. *Swallows and Amazons*. Rev. edn.

Ransome, Arthur 1976. *The Autobiography of Arthur Ransome*. Ed. Rupert Hart-Davis.

Roberts, D. S. 1999. 'Thomas De Quincey's "Danish Origin of the Lake Country Dialect"'. *Transactions of the Cumberland and Westmorland Antiquarian and Archaeological Society*. New Series 99, 257–65.

Shippey, T. A. 1982. *The Road to Middle-earth*.

Size, Nicholas 1929. *The Secret Valley*.

Size, Nicholas 1932. *Shelagh of Eskdale, or, The Stone of Shame*.

Size, Nicholas 1933. *Ola the Russian*.

Snell, K. D. M. 1998. 'The Regional Novel: Themes for Interdisciplinary Research'. In *The Regional Novel in Britain and Ireland, 1800–1990*. Ed. K. D. M. Snell, 1–53.

Ward, Mrs Humphry 1888. *Robert Elsmere*.

Wawn, Andrew 1992. 'The Spirit of 1892: Sagas, Saga-steads and Victorian Philology'. *Saga-Book* 23, 213–52.

Wawn, Andrew 1995. 'Foreword to the 1995 reprint'. In Thomas Ellwood, *Lakeland and Iceland*.

Wawn, Andrew 1997. 'W. G. Collingwood and *Njála*: An Unpublished Poem'. In *Bókahnútur brugðinn Ólöfu Benediktsdóttur fimmtugri, 4. febrúar 1997*, 107–09.

Wawn, Andrew 2000. *The Vikings and the Victorians: Inventing the Old North in Nineteenth-Century Britain*.

Obituaries of W. G. Collingwood:

The Times 3rd October 1932.

Transactions of the Cumberland and Westmorland Antiquarian and Archaeological Society. New Series 33 (1932–33), 308–12.

Obituary of C. A. Parker:

Transactions of the Cumberland and Westmorland Antiquarian and Archaeological Society. New Series 18 (1918), 243–45.

TOLKIEN AND OLD NORSE ANTIQUITY: REAL AND ROMANTIC LINKS IN MATERIAL CULTURE

DIMITRA FIMI

Introduction: Tolkien and the Norse World

For anyone familiar with the Old Norse world and with Tolkien's work, the influences of the one upon the other are manifold and clearly evident. The reasons for this are not just that Tolkien was a philologist specializing in Old English and very well-read in Old Norse, but also that he lived and wrote in a period when the Germanic tradition was indissolubly linked with England's own past. The preoccupation of Britain with its Northern past started in the eighteenth and nineteenth centuries, when scholars re-discovered and started studying texts in vernacular Northern European languages, including Old Norse and Anglo-Saxon, as opposed to the previous veneration of the Classical tradition. This search for English identity in the Norse world was also enhanced by the movement of Romanticism. Tolkien (1892–1973) was proud of his Anglo-Saxon descent, especially the strand of his mother's family. He once wrote to his son Christopher:

> Still I hope one day you'll be able (if you wish) to delve into this intriguing story of the origins of our peculiar people. And indeed of us in particular. For barring the Tolkien (which must long ago have become a pretty thin strand) you are a Mercian and a Hwiccian (of Wychwood) on both sides. (Carpenter 1981, 108)

He viewed England's Anglo-Saxon past as part of a wider whole, including Germany and Scandinavia. In a 1941 letter he praised Northern literature as a world apart from the Classical tradition, writing:

> I have spent most of my life [. . .] studying Germanic matters (in the general sense that includes England and Scandinavia). There is a great deal more force (and truth) [. . .] in the 'Germanic' ideal. I was much attracted by it as an undergraduate [. . .] in reaction against the 'Classics'. (Carpenter 1981, 55)

Tolkien was very young when he encountered the languages and literatures of Northern Europe. Already in his schooldays at King Edward's School in Birmingham he had encountered *Vǫlsunga Saga*. On 17 February 1911, he gave a paper for the Literary Society of the School on 'Norse Sagas'. As the school magazine reports, Tolkien gave a detailed summary of the 'strange and glorious tale' of *Vǫlsunga Saga*, comparing it with Homer's epics, and defending its 'highest epic genius struggling out of savagery'. He also referred to other sagas, and read parts of them in the original (Anon. 1911, 19–20). In Oxford Tolkien started as a student of Classics but he switched to the English School and studied Old Norse and Old English, his syllabus including the *Prose* and *Poetic Eddas*, Norse sagas, and a wide range of Old English texts (see Scull and Hammond 2006, 39–40). In his first academic post in Leeds, Tolkien, together with his colleague E. V. Gordon, played an important role in forming a Viking Club among the undergraduates, which, according to Tolkien's biographer, 'met to drink large quantities of beer, read sagas and sing comic songs' (Carpenter 1977, 105). When he returned to Oxford, Tolkien formed a new informal reading club that met to read Icelandic sagas in the original, the Kolbítar (Coalbiters), meaning 'those who lounge so close to the fire in the winter that they "bite the coal"' (Carpenter 1977, 119–20). C. S. Lewis was introduced to the original sources of the Northern world through this reading club.

The influences of Old Norse texts on Tolkien's creative writing, in terms of motifs, characters, and storylines, are abundant. Some are very evident, like the names of the dwarves in *The Hobbit*, as well as Gandalf's name: these come from the *Dvergatal* in *Vǫluspá*. Another such unmistakable example is Tolkien's tragic hero Túrin Turambar, whose story features in *The Silmarillion* (1977, 198–226). Túrin is a blend of Kullervo from the Finnish *Kalevala* and Sigurðr from *Vǫlsunga Saga* (Shippey 2005, 109–10; Helms 1981, 6–12). Tom Shippey, in his seminal study *The Road to Middle-earth*, has identified and discussed numerous other instances where Tolkien borrows from Old Norse literature, often elaborating on or adapting his source material. Some examples are the dialogue of Bilbo and the dragon Smaug in *The Hobbit*, which is based on the exchanges between Sigurðr and Fáfnir in *Fáfnismál*, and the tale of the Númenórean mariner-king Aldarion and his wife Erendis, which seems to echo the story of Njǫrðr and Skaði in the *Prose Edda* (Shippey 2005, 102, 277–78).[1]

As well as from texts, however, Tolkien seems also to have borrowed from the material culture of the Scandinavian past, real or invented and romanticized. In *The Lord of the Rings* the human culture of Gondor plays an important part in the politics of Middle-earth. Tolkien compared

---

[1] Tolkien's Norse sources are also discussed in Ryan 1966, St Claire 1995a, 1995b, Evans 2000, and most recently Burns 2005.

Gondor with Byzantium in its period of decline, with Rome and the Roman Empire, as well as with ancient Egypt (Carpenter 1981, 157, 376, 281). However, there is enough evidence to suggest that an original source for the culture of Gondor, and of its predecessor, the culture of Númenor, could have been the Vikings.

Ship-burials and the Men of Númenor

The kingdom of Gondor, according to the fictional history of Middle-earth, is only a remnant of the greater and much more majestic lost civilization of Númenor. Tolkien did not create this distinct human culture until the 1930s, when he transformed his 'Atlantis complex'—a recurring dream of a great wave, flooding and engulfing everything around him—into a new version of the Atlantis myth, and thus created the island of Númenor (see Carpenter 1977, 23, 170). According to the mythical history of Middle-earth, at the beginning of the Second Age, the Men who fought by the side of the Elves in the Last Alliance against the evil Vala Morgoth were rewarded by being given as a new dwelling place the Western island of Númenor, and a longer span of life, three times that of other Men. But one command had also been laid upon the Númenóreans, the 'Ban of the Valar': they were forbidden to sail west and attempt to set foot on Valinor, the land of the gods. For though a long life had been granted to them, they still remained mortal. The Númenóreans became very powerful and their island became the place of an advanced human civilization. However, they also started to desire the immortality of the Elves and to complain against the Ban. They rebelled under the evil teaching of Sauron, sailed West in search of the Undying Lands, and thus brought about the Downfall of Númenor: their island was overwhelmed in a cataclysm and sank beneath the sea, killing its inhabitants. The only ones saved were a few faithful Númenóreans who still respected the Valar, and who foresaw the disaster that was to befall Númenor; they set sail in nine ships before the island fell, landed in Middle-earth, and founded the kingdoms of Arnor and Gondor.

The story of Númenor is given in outline in Appendix A of *The Lord of the Rings* (Tolkien 2004, 1033–1044), as well as in more detail in *The Silmarillion* (Tolkien 1977, 259–82). The first emergence of the story, however, was between 1936 and 1937, in two related and mostly unfinished works, published posthumously as 'The Fall of Númenor' and 'The Lost Road' (Tolkien 1987, 11–35, 36–108). The story was further developed and elaborated in another unfinished work that Tolkien started writing between late 1945 and 1946, during the period in which he had temporarily stopped working on *The Lord of the Rings*. This work was to be called 'The Notion Club Papers' and has also been published posthumously in *The History of Middle-earth* series (Tolkien 1992, 145–327). An original idea about the Númenórean civilization was its advanced technology in terms of ships and ship-building. The Númenóreans seem to be pictured as renowned mariners, undertaking long voyages by ship to conquer and explore. This image seems to fit very well with the Vikings, who are associated with legendary ships and naval prowess, not only in the sagas and other Old Norse literature, but in popular imagination too. This can be supported by the first writings of Tolkien on Númenor. In the first sketch of the story, he writes that:

> above all their arts the people of Númenor nourished shipbuilding and sea-craft, and became mariners whose like shall never be again, since the world was diminished. (Tolkien 1987, 14)

Nevertheless, what can securely link the Númenóreans with Scandinavia of the Viking period and earlier is their practice of ship-burial. In the 'original outline' of the Númenor story Tolkien refers to 'their ship-burials, and their great tombs' (Tolkien 1987, 12), and later on, in the first version of 'The Fall of Númenor', he elaborates on this concept and adds:

> And they built mightier houses for their dead than for their living, and endowed their buried kings with unavailing treasure. [...] Wherefore the kingdoms upon the west shores of the Old World became a place of tombs, and filled with ghosts. And in the fantasy of their hearts, and the confusion of legends half-forgotten concerning that which had been, they made for their thought a land of shades. [...] And many deemed this land was in the West, and ruled by the Gods, and in shadow the dead, bearing the shadows of their possessions, should come there [...]. For which reason in after days many of their descendants, or men taught by them, buried their dead in ships and set them in pomp upon the sea by the west coasts of the Old World. (Tolkien 1987, 16–17)

The same ideas about the 'mortuary culture of the Númenóreans', as Christopher Tolkien has called it, are repeated in other versions of 'The Fall of Númenor'. In the later story of 'The Lost Road', Tolkien makes a note of his intention to add a chapter of 'a Norse story of ship-burial' (Tolkien 1987, 13, 25, 28, 77).

It seems, then, that the original conception of Númenor bears great cultural resemblances to the Norse world. Tolkien certainly knew of Norse ship-funerals in textual sources, such as the ship-burial of Scyld described in *Beowulf* (lines 26–52), the cremation on a ship of the body of Baldr in the *Prose Edda* (see Faulkes 1987, 49–50), as well as Ibn

Fadlan's account of a ship funeral and cremation among the Rus (see Montgomery 2000, 12–21). The image of the pagan Viking ship burial was also vivid in the popular imagination of the time, as can be seen, for example, in Francis Dicksee's 1893 painting 'A Funeral of a Viking' (see front cover).

Tolkien could also have had in mind Scandinavian archaeology, however, and especially the ship-burials excavated in Scandinavia in the late nineteenth and early twentieth century. It might be relevant that at the time that Tolkien was writing the earliest Númenórean material, his former colleague in the University of Leeds and very close friend, E. V. Gordon, was just publishing his translation of Shetelig and Falk's *Scandinavian Archaeology* (1937). Tolkien at the time was already in Oxford, and Gordon had moved to the University of Manchester, but they still maintained a very close friendship, seeing each other in Oxford where they both served as examiners from time to time, and also still planning to collaborate in scholarly work (Carpenter 1977, 55; Anderson 2003, 18, 20). The book Gordon translated, and to which he also added some notes, discusses the archaeology of the Scandinavian countries extensively, from prehistoric times up to the Viking age, and also contains numerous pictures from excavations and archaeological finds, including the Oseberg ship, and gives detailed accounts of the boat-graves at Vendel, and of the Oseberg and the Gokstad ships (Shetelig and Falk 1937, 257, 282).

Apart from the references to ship-burials in his early work, Tolkien also produced several drawings of stylized ships which looked like the standard popular depiction of Viking ships during the period, illustrated with decorated prows, usually in the shape of a dragon's head. This image of Viking ships was popular before the Gokstad and Oseberg ships were excavated in 1880 and 1904 respectively, and although illustrators became more concerned with archaeological accuracy later on, this same image persisted (see Wilson 1980, 228). The first map of Middle-earth, associated with 'The Book of Lost Tales' (*c*.1916–18), is a symbolic depiction of Tolkien's cosmology, where the 'Vessel of the Earth' is portrayed as a Viking ship (Tolkien 1983, 84). In a 1928 painting, again associated with his developing mythology, Tolkien drew the 'Halls of Manwë on the Mountains of the World above Faërie'. In the foreground, a ship of the Teleri figures, with a prow in the shape of a swan's neck and head, but it is also 'in general shape and with oars and square sails like Viking ships' (Hammond and Scull 1995, 54, 56). Finally, two more drawings by Tolkien, this time created as possible illustrations for *The Hobbit*, include the same stylized ships: pencil drawings of 'Esgaroth' and 'Lake Town' both include 'Viking' ships, again with a swan's head prow, but this time without any sails (Hammond and Scull 1995, 132–33, 135).

After 1936–37 Tolkien's interest in ship-funerals and burials and in Viking ships seems to have waned. His later Númenórean story, the 'Notion Club Papers', does not contain any references to such matters. This is particularly striking as only two years after Tolkien wrote 'The Lost Road' the Sutton Hoo ship-burial was excavated, arousing much public interest. However, there is an instance of a boat-funeral in *The Lord of the Rings*. When Aragorn, Legolas, and Gimli decide against building a 'cairn' over the dead Boromir, the former says:

> Then let us lay him in a boat with his weapons, and the weapons of his vanquished foes [. . .]. We will send him to the Falls of Rauros and give him to Anduin. The River of Gondor will take care at least that no evil creature dishonours his bones. (Tolkien 2004, 415)

The arrayal of Boromir in the boat for his last trip is described in detail:

> Now they laid Boromir in the middle of the boat that was to bear him away. The grey hood and elven-cloak they folded and placed beneath his head. They combed his long dark hair and arrayed it upon his shoulders. The golden belt of Lórien gleamed about his waist. His helm they set beside him, and across his lap they laid the cloven horn and the hilts and shards of his sword; beneath his feet they put the swords of his enemies. Then fastening the prow to the stern of the other boat, they drew him out into the water. (Tolkien 2004, 416–17)

Although the decision for a boat-funeral, rather than the building of a cairn for Boromir, depends really upon practical issues, since the three remaining members of the fellowship are in need of haste, and such a cairn burial would demand both time and labour (Tolkien 2004, 415), it is significant that Boromir is a man of Gondor, the kingdom of Men on Middle-earth descended from the faithful Númenóreans who were saved from the great flood.

Tolkien's fascination with ship-burials and Viking ships seems to have returned later in his life. Among his manuscripts held at the Bodleian Library in Oxford there are three newspaper clippings, which must have attracted Tolkien's interest. Two clippings concern the 'pseudo-ship-burials' excavated in Norfolk in 1954 (Bodleian, Tolkien A23, fols 56–57). The third concerns the acquisition by the British Museum of a Viking zoomorphic ship ornament (Bodleian, Tolkien A23, fol. 274). In this clipping the ship's figurehead is described as: 'believed to be the only surviving example of the famous zoomorphic, or animal-headed, ornaments, which as we know from references in the Sagas and from representations on tombstones, adorned the Viking ships'. Today, following more research and carbon-14 analysis on the wood, the ship's figurehead is described as 'Provincial Roman or Germanic', as it has been shown to have been carved much earlier than originally thought (see Bruce-Mitford 1974, 175–87).

In addition to the ship-burials, Tolkien compared the material culture of Gondor with Scandinavian archaeology on one further occasion. This was in relation to Fornost, a city of the North Kingdom of the Númenóreans in Middle-earth, Arnor, which was for a while the seat of its kings. In *The Fellowship of the Ring*, Elrond describes Fornost as follows:

> In the North after the war and the slaughter of the Gladden Fields the Men of Westernesse were diminished, and their city of Annúminas beside Lake Evendim fell into ruin; and the heirs of Valandil removed and dwelt at Fornost on the high North Downs, and that now too is desolate. Men call it Deadmen's Dike, and they fear to tread there. For the folk of Arnor dwindled, and their foes devoured them, and their lordship passed, leaving only green mounds in the grassy hills. (Tolkien 2004, 244)

When *The Lord of the Rings* was translated into Swedish in 1961, the translator, Åke Ohlmark, also wrote a biographical introduction on Tolkien, in which he claimed in a humorous way that Tolkien's move from Leeds back to Oxford was for him 'like coming home again from a trial expedition up to the distant "Fornost"' (Carpenter 1981, 305). Tolkien was quite angry about this as well as about other claims of Ohlmark's, and wrote to Allen and Unwin:

> I was devoted to the University of Leeds, which was very good to me, and to the students, whom I left with regret. [. . .] If O[hlmark]'s nonsense was to come to the notice of the University it would give offence, and I would have to publicly apologise. As for 'Fornost', a glance at the book would show that it is comparable rather to the Kings' mounds at Old Uppsala than to the city of Leeds! (Carpenter 1981, 305–06)

The mounds of the Kings at Old Uppsala, in Sweden, are among Scandinavia's most remarkable prehistoric remains, and include three large barrows dated to the fifth and sixth centuries. However, Tolkien's only description of Fornost ('green mounds on the grassy hills') is vague and lacking in any specific detail, so much so that any other European burial site containing mounds or barrows could fit as a source. Tolkien might have chosen the Kings' mounds at Uppsala as a comparison to

Fornost as a Swedish monument that would be familiar to the Swedish translator, and would emphatically convey the image of a landscape of barrows and ancient burial sites in contrast to the city of Leeds. Nevertheless, it is significant that Tolkien thinks of a place in the old kingdom of Gondor in terms of a well-known Scandinavian monument, which again he could have known from Gordon's translation of Shetelig and Falk's book. Indeed, this book refers to the graves of the Kings at Old Uppsala as being 'among the largest monuments in Europe', containing 'three massive barrows', and goes on to describe in detail the boat-burials and the finds from excavations there (Shetelig and Falk 1937, 257–58). In the case of Fornost, then, Tolkien does not refer to ship-burial, but he compares the place with a Scandinavian one that does contain such burials and is regarded as one of the most important sites of the Norse world.

The Valkyrie Helmet and the Crown of Gondor

When one bears in mind the influence of Viking material culture on the civilization of Númenor, one is surprised to find that one more feature that would reinforce this link was specifically denied by Tolkien. This is the helmet and crown of Gondor, both of which are described as having wings. When in 1958 Rhona Beare wrote to Tolkien asking for details on how the 'winged crown' of Gondor looked, comparing it with 'that of a Valkyrie, or as depicted on a Gauloise cigarette packet', Tolkien answered:

> The Númenóreans of Gondor were proud, peculiar, and archaic, and I think are best pictured in (say) Egyptian terms. In many ways they resembled 'Egyptians'—the love of, and power to construct, the gigantic and massive. And in their great interest in ancestry and in tombs. [. . .] I think the crown of Gondor (the S. Kingdom) was very tall, like that of Egypt, but with wings attached, not set straight back but at an angle. The N. Kingdom had only a *diadem* (III 323). Cf. the difference between the N. and S. kingdoms of Egypt. (Carpenter 1981, 281)

Tolkien refers here to the two crowns of Egypt, the *deshret*, or the Red Crown (Fig. 4, right), which was the characteristic headgear of the Pharaoh as King of Lower Egypt (North Kingdom), and the White Crown, the *hedjet* (Fig. 4, left), which was to become the emblematic headgear of the Pharaoh as King of Upper Egypt (South Kingdom) (Aldred 1965, 43–45). Later on, the two crowns were combined in the Double Crown (Fig. 4, middle), which symbolized kingship over the entire country (Redford 2001, 323). Tolkien supplied Rhona

Tolkien and Old Norse Antiquity   91

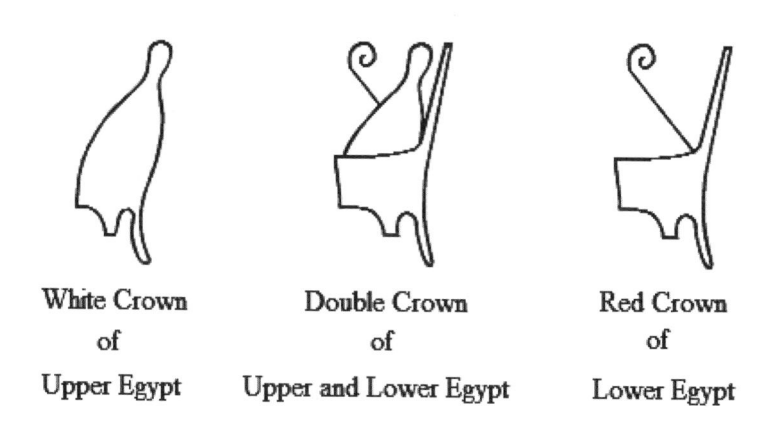

White Crown of Upper Egypt   Double Crown of Upper and Lower Egypt   Red Crown of Lower Egypt

Figure 4: The Crowns of Egypt (© Kevin Brown)

Figure 5: The Crown of Gondor. Illustration from *The Letters of J. R. R. Tolkien*, edited by Humphrey Carpenter with the assistance of Christopher Tolkien (1981), p. 281. © George Allen & Unwin, 1981; reproduced by permission of the Tolkien Estate, HarperCollins Publishers Ltd., and Houghton Mifflin Company. All rights reserved.

Beare with a drawing showing how he visualized the crown of Gondor (Fig. 5).

What is immediately obvious to the reader, then, is that Tolkien assigns to the *North* Kingdom of Gondor a crown that resembles the Crown of the *South* Kingdom of Egypt. Actually the two crowns look identical, save for the wings that the crown of Gondor has as an additional feature. It is not easy to demonstrate whether Tolkien meant to make such an association, or whether his superficial knowledge of Egyptian archaeology is the reason for not identifying the crown of the South Kingdom of Egypt with the crown of the South Kingdom of Gondor, and that of the North Kingdom of Egypt with the crown of the North Kingdom of Gondor. The great resemblance of the crowns pictured in Tolkien's sketch and the Egyptian crowns in Figures 4 and 5 shows that Tolkien had an idea of how the latter looked, and the fact that he refers to the 'difference between the N. and S. kingdoms of Egypt' also shows that he was aware of the two different crown styles. But how much more wide or detailed his knowledge of Egyptian material was cannot be proven. Being in Oxford he could easily have been exposed to books or even lectures and photographs concerning excavations and finds in Egypt, but no conclusive evidence exists.

However, this rejection of the idea that the crown of Gondor resembles anything Norse is suspicious. For somebody with Tolkien's academic background, the most straightforward association of the crown of Gondor would be with the headgear of the valkyries, as his reader pointed out, although the winged helmet and its association with the Vikings was the product of romanticism and not based on any historical or archaeological data. The winged and the horned helmets of romanticized Vikings seem to have been established by the tradition of the costumes used in Wagner's operas, while their prototypes possibly originated in a confusion of Viking and Celtic helmets, the latter's winged forms themselves having sprung from classical images, such as that of Hermes (see Frank 2000, Langer 2002 and Wilson 1980, 214, 227, 231). Nevertheless, the depiction of Norse heroes and deities with winged helmets alongside horned ones was commonplace in post-Wagnerian visual culture, as Figures 6 and 7 show. The costumes of Wagner's operas, especially of *Der Ring des Nibelungen*, played an important role in standardizing the image of the Viking deities or heroes with highly decorated helmets.

Tolkien describes the crown of Gondor as a more lavish version of the helmet of Gondor. When Gandalf and Pippin arrive in Minas Tirith in Book VI of *The Lord of the Rings*, they see that:

The Guards of the gate were robed in black, and their helms were of strange shape, high-crowned, with long cheek-guards close-fitting to the face, and above the cheek-guards were set the white wings of sea-birds; but the helms gleamed with a flame of silver, for they were indeed wrought of *mithril*, heirlooms from the glory of old days. (Tolkien 2004, 752–53)

Figure 6: *The Chosen Slain* (artist: K. Dielitz), in Guerber 1908, 18

Figure 7: *Odin and Brunhild* (artist: K. Dielitz), in Guerber 1908, 280

Tolkien's fullest description of Gondor's crown is found in the account of Aragorn's coronation:

Then the guards stepped forward, and Faramir opened the casket, and he held up an ancient crown. It was shaped like the helms of the Guards of the Citadel, save that it was loftier, and it was all white, and the wings at either side were wrought of pearl and silver in the likeness of the wings of a sea-bird, for it was the emblem of kings who came over the Sea; and seven gems of adamant were set in the circlet, and upon its summit was set a single jewel the light of which went up like a flame. (Tolkien 2004, 967)

Indeed, in another instance where Tolkien made a drawing of the crown, its depiction certainly brings to mind the romantic Valkyrie helmet, rather than the White and Red Crowns of Egypt. This was in one

Figure 8: The Winged Crown of Gondor
Bodleian Library, Oxford, MS. Tolkien Drawings 90, fol. 30. © The Tolkien Estate, reproduced by permission of the Tolkien Estate and the Bodleian Library, Oxford.

of the dust-jacket designs that Tolkien drew for the third volume of *The Lord of the Rings*, but which was too expensive to reproduce (Hammond and Scull 1995, 183). The winged crown is found in the middle of the drawing, which has been reproduced as Figure 8.

Finally, in his very early work 'The Book of Lost Tales', Tolkien had referred to a people he calls the 'Winged Helms', their other name being the 'Forodwaith', in association with the story of Aelfwine of England (Tolkien 1984, 330, 334). In that story Tolkien constructs a pseudo-history of England, and its successive invasions by different peoples. Christopher Tolkien has pointed out that 'the Forodwaith are of course Viking invaders from Norway or Denmark' (Tolkien 1984, 323). It seems, then, that (at least in his early writings) Tolkien himself would associate winged helmets or winged crowns with Norse culture, and not with the crowns of Egypt.

A possible explanation of this discrepancy is Tolkien's reaction to World War II. The appropriation of the 'Germanic ideal' by Nazi Germany was a source of aggravation for Tolkien. In the 1941 letter quoted above, he continues:

> Anyway, I have in this War a burning private grudge [. . .] against that ruddy little ignoramus Adolf Hitler [. . .]. *Ruining, perverting, misapplying, and making for ever accursed, that noble northern spirit*, a supreme contribution to Europe, which I have ever loved, and tried to present in its true light. (Carpenter 1981, 55–56, emphasis added)[2]

The exaltation of the Northern past would not have gone down well in post-World War II Britain. In addition, the memory of the controversial position of some Scandinavian countries during the war could have made things even worse. This might also explain why Tolkien suddenly stopped mentioning ship-burials in his stories of Númenor before and during the war, despite the spectacular discovery of the Sutton Hoo ship-burial, which could have—under different circumstances—strengthened such references. At the same time, though, by comparing Númenor with Egypt, Tolkien might also have played on the contrast between ancient archaeology, including Egypt and classical Greece (an archaeology with majestic and imposing remains, denoting a 'highly civilised' culture), and that of northern Europe, which has much less magnificent and readily recognizable archaeology to display, something that leads

---

[2] For a comparison of Tolkien's use of Germanic myth and legend and that of the Nazis, and a discussion of Tolkien's reactions to Nazi Germany, see Chism 2003.

to it being associated with a more 'primitive' culture (which for Tolkien would also mean a 'purer' and 'nobler' one). Surely, in that case, Gondor would be the classical civilization in decline, and that would make a sharp contrast with the Anglo-Saxon culture of Rohan (see Tolkien 2004, 1136, Shippey 2005, 139–45 and Shippey 2001, 90–97) and its more 'primitive' society.

Epilogue: Filming Tolkien's Norse Materiality

Tolkien's use of the material culture of the Vikings and pre-Viking Scandinavia is an element of Middle-earth that can be easily missed, having been too well hidden or played down by Tolkien himself. As discussed above, this 'borrowed' Viking materiality is not only associated with real archaeological finds, but, as we have seen, is also based on misconceptions and romanticized interpretations of past civilizations. The winged helmet of Gondor is such a case, but so also is the fascination with ship-burials and Viking ships in popular imagination. Tolkien might have known more about Scandinavian archaeology through his contact with E. V. Gordon, but he was not an archaeologist himself, and his response to archaeology was more emotional than academic. Where Tolkien's Middle-earth is concerned, it is more the romantic envisioning of a remote heroic past that appeals to the reader, rather than any accuracy in the depiction of the cultures of the peoples of Middle-earth or their modelling upon real historical cultures. Tolkien's admiration for the Norse world is evident not only in his use of texts, motifs and stories, but in inventing a culture that—at least to an average, non-specialist reader—would have a Norse feel to it, incorporating both authentic material and romantic fabrications. And this is significant when one bears in mind that Tolkien argued on occasion that Middle-earth is not really an imaginary place but Northern Europe in a very remote past back in human prehistory (Carpenter 1981, 239, 376). It is only natural then that a human culture echoing Old Norse antiquity would be present, as it also makes sense that an Anglo-Saxon human culture would also appear (see Shippey 2001, 90–102).

Interestingly, the two film adaptations of *The Lord of the Rings* have chosen to deal with the Viking materiality of Gondor in different ways. In Ralph Bakshi's animated adaptation (1978), Boromir is pictured as a stereotyped Viking, with a fur tunic and a horned helmet. His funeral is much closer to the romanticized Viking funerals too: the little boat he is placed in has a dragon-head prow, his body is covered, and the horned helmet is placed upon it. To make the Viking associations even clearer, the filmmakers have added a set of four burning torches on the boat, although we do not see the boat burning, but just sailing slowly on the river. In Peter Jackson's version (2001–03), the Viking elements are rather played down. Boromir's funeral is an iconic moment, but the film follows Tolkien very closely, and does not employ additional Viking overtones. In contrast, when it comes to the winged helmets and crown of Gondor, the filmmakers seem anxious to avoid such connotations. The Gondorian helmet of the Second Age, as briefly seen in the prologue of *The Fellowship of the Ring* (2001), has metal wings, but shaped and designed in such a way as not to draw attention to them. In the Third Age helmet, as seen mainly in *The Return of the King* (2003), the wings are imprinted on the surface of the helmet, and are very easy to overlook. What appears to have been a headache for the design team was the helmet of the guards of the gate in Gondor. As the quotation above shows, Tolkien described those helmets very specifically as being winged. In the 'Appendices' of the extended DVD edition of *The Return of the Kings*, the two main conceptual designers of the design team (and also well-known Tolkien illustrators before their participation in the film), Alan Lee and John Howe, discuss the problem of the winged helmets. Alan Lee points out that with Tolkien's description 'you immediately think of Vikings', although he goes on to assert that it would really be a romanticized image of a Viking. John Howe calls the whole affair of the winged helmets 'an annoying idea', which spoils the aesthetic of Middle-earth, and he adds 'that would be heartbreaking to see all of these Gondorians hopping about in Thor helmets, wouldn't it?'. Their eventual solution does not overcome the problem of Viking associations, since the helmets figure two enormous sets of wings, but the Guards are shown only once in the whole film, and the shot is very brief, as if the viewer is actually encouraged to forget about this whole sorry affair.

Tolkien's creation of the Númenóreans' Gondorian materiality is one more tribute to the Norse world, and one more attempt to root his mythology in the Old North and its legends. Tolkien's initial impetus for writing his legendarium was his romantic project to create a 'mythology for England', associated with England's Anglo-Saxon past (see Shippey 2001, x–xvi; Drout 2004). This is also why he insisted on using the term 'England' rather than 'Britain', since the latter term conveys the historical result of all ethnic groups that inhabited the British Isles in the past, including the Celts and Normans. Since Tolkien viewed the Anglo-

Saxons as the 'real' ancestors of the English, then the natural ancestors of the Anglo-Saxons, the Germanic peoples, also had to be represented in his mythology. The ship-burials and winged helmets of the people of Númenor and Gondor place them securely—at least in the sphere of popular imagination—within the cultural milieu of Viking and earlier Scandinavian material culture, and offer a new perception of the Norse world in one of the most influential works of modern fantasy.

Bibliography

Aldred, Cyril 1965. *Egypt to the End of the Old Kingdom*.
Anderson, Douglas A. 2003. '"An Industrious Little Devil": E. V. Gordon as friend and collaborator with Tolkien'. In *Tolkien the Medievalist*. Ed. Jane Chance, 15–25.
Anon. 1911. 'Literary Society'. *King Edward's School Chronicle* 26 (186): 19–22.
Bakshi, Ralph, dir., 1978. *The Lord of the Rings*.
Bruce-Mitford, Rupert 1974. *Aspects of Anglo-Saxon Archaeology: Sutton Hoo and Other Discoveries*.
Burns, Marjorie 2005. *Perilous Realms: Celtic and Norse in Tolkien's Middle-earth*.
Carpenter, Humphrey 1977. *Tolkien: A Biography*.
Carpenter, Humphrey, ed., 1981. *The Letters of J. R. R. Tolkien: A Selection*.
Chism, Christine 2003. 'Middle-earth, the Middle Ages, and the Aryan Nation: Myth and History in World War II'. In *Tolkien the Medievalist*. Ed. Jane Chance, 63–92.
Drout, Michael D. C. 2004. 'A Mythology for Anglo-Saxon England'. In *J. R. R. Tolkien and the Invention of Myth: A Reader*. Ed. Jane Chance, 335–62.
Evans, Jonathan. 2000. 'The Dragon-Lore of Middle-earth: Tolkien and Old English and Old Norse Tradition'. In *J. R. R. Tolkien and His Literary Resonances: Views of Middle-earth*. Ed. George Clark and Daniel Patrick Timmons, 21–38.
Faulkes, Anthony, trans., 1987. Snorri Sturluson. *Edda*.
Frank, Roberta 2000. 'The Invention of the Viking Horned Helmet'. In *International Scandinavian and Medieval Studies in Memory of Gerd Wolfgang Weber: Ein runder Knaüel, so rollt' es uns leicht aus den Händen*. Ed Michael Dallapiazza, Olaf Hansen, Preben Meulengracht Sørensen, and Yvonne S. Bonnetain, 199–208.
Guerber, H. A. 1908. *Myths of the Norsemen from the Eddas and Sagas*.
Hammond, Wayne G., and Christina Scull, eds, 1995. *J. R. R. Tolkien: Artist & Illustrator*.
Helms, Randel 1981. *Tolkien and the Silmarils*.
Jackson, Peter, dir., 2001. *The Lord of the Rings: The Fellowship of the Ring*. Extended DVD edition.
Jackson, Peter, dir., 2003. *The Lord of the Rings: The Return of the King*. Extended DVD edition.

Langer, Johnni 2002. 'The Origins of the Imaginary Viking'. *Viking Heritage Magazine* 4, 6–9.
Montgomery, James E. 2000. 'Ibn Fadlan and the Rusiyyah'. *Journal of Arabic and Islamic Studies* 3, 1–25.
Redford, Donald B., ed., 2001. *The Oxford Encyclopedia of Ancient Egypt*. 3 vols.
Ryan, J. S. 1966. 'German Mythology Applied: The Extension of Literary Folk Memory'. *Folklore* 77 (1): 45–59.
Scull, Christina, and Wayne G. Hammond 2006. *The J. R. R. Tolkien Companion and Guide, Volume I: Chronology*.
Shetelig, Haakon and Hjalmar Falk 1937. *Scandinavian Archaeology*. Trans. E. V. Gordon.
Shippey, T. A. 2001. *J. R. R. Tolkien: Author of the Century*.
Shippey, T. A. 2005. *The Road to Middle-earth*. Revised and expanded edn.
St. Claire, Gloriana 1995a. 'An Overview of Northern Influences on Tolkien's Work'. In *Proceedings of the J. R. R. Tolkien Centenary Conference, 1992*. Ed. Patricia Reynolds and Glen GoodKnight, 63–67.
St. Claire, Gloriana 1995b. '*Volsunga Saga* and *Narn*: Some Analogies'. In *Proceedings of the J. R. R. Tolkien Centenary Conference, 1992*. Ed. Patricia Reynolds and Glen GoodKnight, 68–72.
Tolkien, J. R. R. 1977. *The Silmarillion*. Ed. Christopher Tolkien.
Tolkien, J. R. R. 1983. *The Book of Lost Tales: Part I*. Ed. Christopher Tolkien.
Tolkien, J. R. R. 1984. *The Book of Lost Tales: Part II*. Ed. Christopher Tolkien.
Tolkien, J. R. R. 1987. *The Lost Road and Other Writings: Language and Legend Before The Lord of the Rings*. Ed. Christopher Tolkien.
Tolkien, J. R. R. 1992. *Sauron Defeated*. Ed. Christopher Tolkien.
Tolkien, J. R. R. 2004. *The Lord of the Rings*. Ed. Wayne G. Hammond and Christina Scull. 50th anniversary edn.
Wilson, David M. 1980. *The Northern World: The History and Heritage of Northern Europe, AD 400–1100*.

FROM RUNIC INSCRIPTIONS TO RUNIC GYMNASTICS

HEATHER O'DONOGHUE

In 1936 the German occultist Friedrich Bernhard Marby, inventor of *Runengymnastik* ('runic gymnastics'), was sentenced to imprisonment by the Third Reich because his particular brand of mystic nationalism was denounced as an anti-Nazi activity. He ended up in Dachau. In this essay I hope to trace how the runic alphabet, especially as understood in relation to Old Norse mythology, came to be associated with a bizarre form of twentieth-century occultism which went beyond even National Socialism's tolerance of Nordic revivalism.

What we now call 'Norse mythology' is very largely encoded in texts which were written down in medieval Iceland. In its written form, then—and whatever its origins—it belongs, indisputably, to Iceland itself. However, the thriving settlement of medieval Iceland, which had been uniquely productive in literary terms, suffered a very severe decline in the early modern period. For a number of reasons, amongst them climate change, internal instability, colonization, and the politics of mainland Scandinavia, Iceland became isolated, culturally as well as geographically, and texts written in Iceland in the Middle Ages—a huge repository of literature, including mythological texts and treatises—were for a time lost to the wider European world. Given that Iceland had become a Danish colony, it is not surprising that it was at first Danish scholars who began to seek out Icelandic material which seemed to offer so much valuable information about the early history and culture of the Scandinavian peoples (and it was believed then that some of this material was extremely ancient—very much earlier than scholars nowadays suppose). Scholars such as Ole Worm or Wormius (1636) and Peder Hansen Resen or Resenius (1665, facsimile in Faulkes 1977) wrote on and published Old Icelandic texts—crucially, in Latin, and with Latin translations, thus ensuring their dissemination throughout all of learned Europe, including Britain.

But the Swedes too had been pursuing their ancient national past, and two scholars in particular, Johannes Magnus and Olaus Rudbeck, are celebrated for their construction of elaborate, self-flattering, and largely fantastic accounts of this ancient 'history'. In the sixteenth century, Johannes Magnus in his *Historia [. . .] de omnibus Gothorum*

Sveonumque regibus (1554) had identified the Swedes with the descendants of Magog, Noah's grandson, who had side-stepped the confusion of Babel and had thus retained the original language of mankind, God's own tongue. Towards the end of the seventeenth century, in his book *Atlantica,* Rudbeck claimed that the origin of the Swedish nation was Atlantis, the birthplace of all European civilization.[1] According to Johannes Magnus, as well as besieging Rome, toppling Troy, and teaching philosophy to Plato, these ancient Swedes had also created a great literature. This literature had, it was claimed, been written originally in runes, the ancient Germanic alphabet. There were, after all, remnants of this writing—in the form of barely legible inscriptions on stone—throughout northern Europe. The Roman alphabet, so the theory went, was a papal plot, designed to suppress this pre-Christian native Germanic culture. In this way, runes, and runic inscriptions, came to be regarded as the last traces of a great, lost, Scandinavian, pre-Christian, civilization.

Old Icelandic texts came to be venerated as precious written survivals of this lost civilization, especially in their accounts on the one hand of Old Norse myth, held to be an authentic reflection of ancient Scandinavian religion and culture, and on the other, of early Scandinavian history. (It is ironic that those texts which were first taken to provide historical information—the *fornaldarsögur*, most often set in a legendary Scandinavian pre-history—are precisely those which are nowadays understood as the most fictional, not to say fantastic.) The Danish scholar Ole Worm also believed that Icelandic texts had originally been written in runes, and laboriously transliterated the texts he quoted in his appendix to *Literatura runica*. Peder Resen, thankfully, did not.

Both Worm and Resen believed in the extreme antiquity of the literature, the language and the runic alphabet, but runes themselves were seen primarily as an ancient script, a vehicle for textuality. Nonetheless, the association of runes with pagan magic is a long-standing one. Nowadays, runes are popularly associated with divination—either in the political, journalistic sense, 'reading the runes' being a cliché for having an informed understanding of what news may be about to break; or in New Age, mystical circles, in which runes seem to have replaced tarot cards as fashionable instruments for fortune-telling. But apart from an obscure reference in the *Germania*, in which Tacitus claims that the Germanic tribes predicted the future by means of small sticks with marks

---

[1] The place of Johannes Magnus in Swedish historiography is well explained by Roberts 1979, together with a succinct account of his ideas. For an account of Rudbeck's theories, see Malm 1994.

on them (Hutton 1970, 144–45),[2] runes have not until recently been credited with clairvoyant properties. On the other hand, authors of Old Icelandic texts repeatedly presented runes as having magical properties, and actual runic inscriptions have been reliably understood by modern scholars as recording magic formulae (though many have been *un*reliably identified as such).[3]

Runic characters, which have been dated as early as the first century AD, were in fact used for inscriptions of all sorts. It has been argued that the distinctively angular shape of each runic letter originally served to facilitate carving on the grained surface of wood, though surviving inscriptions—for obvious practical reasons—are more often on stone or bone. That many runic inscriptions have survived on substantial monuments or valuable small items—again for obvious reasons—has no doubt contributed to the sense that the runic alphabet itself was in some way portentous. But there are two important counter-weights to this view. As Birgit Sawyer notes, 'scholars agree that most rune-stones are Christian monuments'—Christian gravestones with runic inscriptions, the wording of the inscription being a conventional Christian piety about the soul or God's mercy (Sawyer 2000, 125). In England, an inscription corresponding to part of a poem in Old English which has come to be known as *The Dream of the Rood*—a vision of the cross on which Christ was crucified—was carved on to an eighth-century stone cross in runic lettering (Swanton 1970). Even more dramatically, a relatively recent find of runic inscriptions, mostly on wood, in a medieval cellar in Bergen (since followed by a number of similar finds elsewhere in Norway), makes it quite clear that the runic alphabet could be used for all manner of sometimes trivial domestic and commercial texts: price tags, shopping lists, business letters (see Liestøl 1968 and 1974). An inscription inside a church on the Swedish island of Oland might stand as an example of the range of non-magical, non-pagan, non-portentous runic inscriptions. Dating from about the year AD 1500, it has many of the qualities of modern graffiti: it playfully tells any reader that given the name of the church—Runsten—one might expect its parish priest to be an expert in reading and writing runes. Its author may have been the parish priest himself.[4]

Runologists have been accused of interpreting all obscure runic inscriptions as magical formulae. Certainly, there are indecipherable

---

[2] Hutton notes tersely of these marks: 'Too early for runes' (1970, 144).
[3] See McKinnell and Simek 2004, especially their warning against the uncritical assumption that runic inscriptions must be magical in some way (31).
[4] For the story of this inscription see Brate 1928, 104–05.

sequences of runic letters. We should not automatically assume that these are magical, however. Perhaps they were simply mistakes—what Seamus Heaney, in a poem about Viking carvings in a museum, ominously called 'trial pieces' ('Viking Dublin: Trial Pieces', in Heaney 1975), and we might more prosaically identify as practice inscriptions by apprentice runecarvers. Perhaps they are meaningless doodles, or even purely decorative in function, like the Chinese or Japanese characters on European silks or porcelain. But there is no doubt that some runic inscriptions do encode magic formulae—though again, given that the practice of magic invariably involves language—spells, magic words, curses, and so on—and that any alphabet is a vehicle for language, we might expect some inscriptions to be magical, especially given the pre-Christian origins of the runic alphabet.

Nevertheless, where runes are mentioned in Old Icelandic texts, the context is invariably one of mystery and sorcery. I want to look closely at a few of the most celebrated instances of this, with a view to considering how authentically these accounts might reflect actual magical practices. Without doubt the most celebrated is the account in the eddic poem *Hávamál* of how Óðinn, god of poetry and the dead, gained access to the wisdom of the underworld, and learnt runes. And it is of the greatest importance to the whole story of runic gymnastics that *Hávamál* was one of the first Old Icelandic texts to gain currency in post-medieval Europe: the seventeenth-century scholar Peder Resen published it as an appendix to his edition and Latin translation of the *Prose Edda*.

Towards the end of *Hávamál*, a speaking voice which scholars have unanimously identified as the god Óðinn himself describes how he hung for nine nights on a windswept tree—perhaps the World Tree, Yggdrasill (Óðinn-steed). His agony is disturbingly reminiscent of Christ on the cross (Evans 1986, st. 139):

> Við hleifi mik sældu
> né við hornigi.
>
> No bread did they give me
> nor drink.

Óðinn continues:

> Nam ek upp rúnar,
> œpandi nam,
> fell ek aptr þaðan.
>
> I took up runes
> took [them] screaming
> I fell back from there.

The verbal phrase *nema upp* is tantalizingly imprecise: 'to take up', or 'to pick up', either literally or metaphorically. But it was enough to persuade seventeenth-century antiquarian scholars—including, as early as 1630, the distinguished British historian, Sir Henry Spelman, who had been engaged in a scholarly correspondence with Ole Worm—that Óðinn could be credited with *inventing* runes, especially given that there was a pervasive early and lasting confusion around the adjective 'runic' as qualifying both the alphabet and ancient Scandinavian poetry itself.[5]

Hávamál continues with Óðinn's account of how he learnt *fimbulljóð níu* ('nine mighty spells') from his maternal uncle, the giant Bǫlþórr, and secured a drink of the mythical mead of poetry. A little further on—and perhaps the speaking voice changes here—*Hávamál* tells us more about the runes, directing the reader or listener to find a great and powerful letter made by the powerful gods and carved by *Hroptr rǫgna*—probably a circumlocution for Óðinn himself. And further on again, the poet details several aspects of rune-carving, in the form of an incantatory interrogation of the audience's skill and experience (st. 144):

> Veiztu hvé rísta skal?
> Veiztu hvé ráða skal?
> Veiztu hvé fá skal?
> Veiztu hvé freista skal?
> Veiztu hvé biðja skal?
> Veiztu hvé blóta skal?
> Veiztu hvé senda skal?
> Veiztu hvé sóa skal?

Do you know how to: carve, interpret, stain, test, ask, worship, send, sacrifice?

There follow eighteen spells with various objectives: to combat anxiety, to promote healing, to overcome enemies, to seduce women. And slipped in at number twelve, a distinctly Odinic talent (st. 157):

> ef ek sé á tré uppi
> váfa virgilná,
> svá ek ríst
> ok í rúnum fák
> at sá gengr gumi
> ok mælir við mik.

---

[5] The classic account of the interaction of British scholars and Scandinavian antiquarians is Seaton 1935. See also Quinn and Clunies Ross 1994.

> If I see, up in a tree,
> a hanged corpse dangling,
> I so carve
> and stain in runes
> that the person walks
> and talks to me.

There would seem to be plenty of material here for establishing the link between Óðinn, magic, mystical otherworld wisdom, and runes.

While the wilder reaches of Old Norse myth came to thrill and inspire some fashionable English *literati* in the eighteenth century (see Finlay and Larrington in this volume), the dominant position taken by most scholars on the identity of Óðinn himself followed the line taken by Snorri in his *Prose Edda*, and disseminated by Resen's Latin edition: that Óðinn was not originally a divine figure, but a semi-historical personage who had led his people out of southern Asia northwards into Scandinavia, and who had been subsequently deified by that people. But this still did not undermine the possibility of runic magic. Thus Robert Sheringham, using Resen's text, quotes *Hávamál* and explains that it was the employment of runes for magic purposes which had led to the suppression of them and their literature by the Christian Church, and Sir William Temple put forward the thesis that the magic use of runes was a cunning plan on the part of the old poets 'to Gain and establish the credit and Admiration of their Rhymes'. Interestingly, Temple also advanced the proposition that individual runes had individual magical properties (see Seaton 1935, 230).

Much Old Icelandic poetry was first written down long after its composition—how long is not always known. *Hávamál* has been called by one of its modern editors 'a confusing, even bewildering, work' (Evans 1986, 4): he declared it 'inconceivable' that its 164 strophes constitute one whole poem (Evans 1986, 7). Careful reading of the relevant stanzas shows that the association of runes and magic with Óðinn is not as straightforward as has been assumed—the eighteen spells, for example, are not all necessarily runic. *Hávamál* was, however, very influential when Old Norse myth was reaching its wider audience from the seventeenth century on, however imperfectly it was interpreted.

Other references to rune magic in Old Icelandic poetry may well reflect some knowledge or memory of actual practice. In the poem *Skírnismál* its primary speaker, Skírnir, an emissary sent by the god Freyr to woo the giant maiden Gerðr, threatens her with all kinds of physical, mental and sexual violence, including the threat that he will carve the Þ rune at her

(Dronke 1997, st. 36). The name of this rune in Old Norse is *þurs*, which means 'ogre', and in the Old Icelandic rune poem, in which each of the individual runic characters is given a name, and a brief explanation, Þ is described as *kvenna kvǫl*—'the torment of women' (Page 1998, 5). The verse in *Skírnismál* may refer to the Þ rune being carved three times, to intensify its power; some surviving runic inscriptions consist of a repeated single character, perhaps for the same reason, such as the repeated inscription of the T rune, *týr*, 'victory', carved on the blade of a sword (McKinnell and Simek 2004, 33).

The eddic poem *Sigrdrífumál*, which recounts an exchange between the hero Sigurðr and a valkyrie, Sigrdrífa, includes a detailed section on rune magic, in which the valkyrie instructs Sigurðr, apparently to reward him for freeing her from a Sleeping Beauty-like spell which Óðinn has cast (Neckel 1962, 14–19). Sigrdrífa lists a series of runes useful for all sorts of different purposes: victory-runes, ale-runes, helping-runes (for women in childbirth), sea-runes (for safe voyages), limb-runes, speech-runes, and mind-runes (for unsurpassed wisdom). It may be that even in this poem, whose date is unknown, the information about rune magic is already a little uncertain. The function of 'ale-runes', for example, is not very clearly set out: their usefulness 'if you do not want another's wife to beguile your trust' does not seem to have a great deal to do with ale, although the instruction which follows is to carve these runes on a horn. It is possible that the poet has misunderstood the obscure but apparently powerful runic name *alu* for 'ale' (McKinnell and Simek 2004, 35).

References in the Old Icelandic Family Sagas to the carving of runes for magical purposes are even less to be trusted as transmitting reliable information about authentic practice. In *Egils saga*, which is set in the period before the Conversion of Iceland, the pagan poet Egill Skalla-Grímsson is the planned victim of a poisoning attempt—with poisoned ale, significantly enough. But before he drinks the deadly brew, he carves runes on its horn container, and having drawn blood in the palm of his hand, smears his runes with it. The horn shatters, and the poison spills harmlessly to the floor (Nordal 1933, ch. 44). This episode is built around one of Egill's verses, quoted in the text, and the prose echoes the verse quite closely, suggesting that the anecdote was itself inferred from the verse. If the stanza is indeed older than the saga prose (as many scholars assume, although without certainty), it could be that Egill (or its author) knew the same slightly confused tradition of ale-runes represented in *Sigrdrífumál*—or even, conceivably, the poem (or a version of it) itself.

There is no reason to assume that the saga author knew anything about the actual practice of runic magic.

Further on in *Egils saga*, Egill comes across a farmer whose daughter is very ill (Nordal 1933, ch. 72). Her father explains that a neighbour has carved healing runes for her. Egill finds a runic inscription on a piece of whalebone under the girl's bed, and at once sees that the runes have been miscarved, and are making her ill instead of better. He burns the offending bit of bone, and recarves the inscription, which he places under her pillow. The girl recovers at once. This story functions as a warning against inexperienced rune carvers, and the damage they can inflict. Again, the narrative prose draws very closely on a quoted stanza, and almost presents Egill—the pagan poet—in the role of miraculous healer. Indeed, both episodes betray hagiographical influence: Bjarni Einarsson detected an analogue to the story of the poisoned horn in a legend of St Benedict in Gregory's *Dialogues*, and one to the magic healing episode in the Gospels (1975, 176 and 257–59), and closer comparisons (where it is the writing that cures the sick girl) can be found in similar miracle stories in European saints' lives.[6]

A celebrated instance of malicious rune-magic occurs in *Grettis saga* (Guðni Jónsson 1936, ch. 79). Grettir's enemies are frustrated by the fact that they cannot get at him in his fastness on Drangey, and enlist the help of an old woman, who carves blood-smeared runes on a log which is pushed out to sea so that it will drift ashore on Drangey:

> Hon lét telgja á lítinn flatveg, þar gniðat var; síðan tók hon kníf sinn ok reist rúnar á rótinni ok rauð í blóði sínu ok kvað yfir galdra. Hon gekk ǫfug andsœlis um tréit ok hafði þar yfir mǫrg rǫmm ummæli.

> Where it [the log] had been rubbed smooth, she had a small flat area carved out; then she took her knife and carved runes on the root, and reddened [them] with her blood, and recited spells over them. She walked backwards withershins around the log, and chanted many powerful utterances over it.

When the log is indeed washed up on the shore of Drangey, Grettir twice rejects it as *Illt tré ok af illum sent* ('an evil log, sent by an evil person'), but his lazy servant eventually drags it home, and Grettir hacks at it for firewood without noticing. This careful delay with its third-time-lucky structure suggests the inexorable progress of the supernaturally charged log, and the inevitability of the witch's success. And yet, the saga author neatly side-steps the obvious direct connexion between the

---

[6] For instance, Jerome's Life of Hilarion (White 1998, 99–100). I am indebted to Dr Siân Grønlie for this reference.

witch's runes and Grettir's demise. As he chops the log, Grettir's axe glances off the wood and slices into his leg. But nothing untoward ensues until three nights later, when the wound understandably turns septic and Grettir becomes fatally enfeebled. The significant point here is that the saga audience does not need to believe that it was the supernatural power of the runes which led to Grettir's downfall; the axe wound and the ensuing infection are enough in themselves to motivate the narrative. And whether or not a contemporary or near-contemporary audience liked to believe in the efficacy of runic magic, the saga author has carefully avoided committing himself.

This concludes the first part of this essay—an account of how there came to be clustered around the runic alphabet a powerful mix of ideas. We have a pervasive, if somewhat insecurely based, association between runes and magical wisdom. We have the antiquarian thrill of runic inscriptions as the traces of a great, long-lost European culture. We have, on the margins, the Church understood as an adversary of this culture. This was to prove an irresistible package for later romantic nationalists with a mystical bent and some grounds for association with Scandinavian culture—that is to say, those German-speaking proponents of mystic nationalism who paved the way to the horrors of Nazi racism on the one hand, and the relatively harmless delights of runic gymnastics on the other.

The rise of German romantic nationalism in the nineteenth century has been thoroughly documented by historians (Breuilly 1992, Scales and Zimmer 2005, Geary 2002). Bolstered by the new science of Indo-European philology, it could claim that nationality depended to some extent on language, and that therefore those who spoke German—or, a crucial extension, some form of the readily apparent group of 'Germanic' languages—could identify themselves as belonging to a single, 'pan-Germanic', nation. This identification was further confirmed by new theories about race—the idea that certain physical and mental characteristic could define a people—in this case, the so-called 'Nordic type', characterized as it happened by superior physical and mental features, and like their language, supposedly untainted by admixture, especially from the despised Mediterranean or Semitic nations. And the ancient origin of this newly defined and superior people was well established: as far back as Tacitus in the first century AD, a Germanic ethnicity had been recognized (and praised).

All that remained was to link the origins of the Germanic peoples to Scandinavian pre-history. The place of the Scandinavian languages in the Germanic group was indisputable. All of them could be traced back to a form of 'Proto-Germanic' original. The theory that the Scandinavians—including the Icelanders—were descendants of an originally Germanic people was widespread. Icelandic texts such as the *Edda* thus miraculously preserved the ancient culture of the German nation—preserved it because, as refugees from early Christian persecution, its authors had escaped northwards, into Scandinavia, and even as far as Iceland. Old Norse myth—and with it, runes and all their associations—came to be regarded as the cultural heart of the new idea of a pan-Germanic nation. To study Old Norse myth and runic lore was to connect with this cultural heart, and, in the view of its most extreme practitioners, to cause it to beat again.

A key figure here is Guido von List, a German-speaking Austrian nationalist who not only adopted this whole package of ideas, but also significantly advanced the pseudo-science of runic mysticism. Born in 1848, even as a teenager von List allied himself with what he believed was Germanic paganism, abandoning his family's Catholicism, and immersing himself in Germanic folklore and legendary history. Von List is credited with inventing ariosophy—a potent blend of theosophy, as popularized by Madame Blavatsky and her followers, and racism: ariosophy was thus the ancient mystical wisdom of the Aryan peoples.[7] Theosophy, which became immensely popular throughout Europe, was a fantastic and all-encompassing setting out of cycles of mystical history which claimed to connect with the philosophy and wisdom of the most ancient and superior races of mankind. Von List and his followers matched Old Norse creation myths with Blavatsky's cosmological cycles, and identified their own Germanic roots with the Aryan races, as Blavatsky defined them, yearning to share in their supposed wisdom, suppressed, as was believed, by the enmity of the early Christian Church, but surviving in Norse myth, and encoded in runes.

Von List's theories about the survival of a supposedly original Germanic culture not only in Norse myths, but also in place-names, monuments, and folk customs throughout Austria might be regarded as harmless, deluded antiquarianism. He believed that it was possible to uncover evidence of temples dedicated to the gods of the Old Norse (that is to say, originally ancient Germanic) pantheon, throughout Europe, even though their names had been cunningly changed to

---

[7] Blavatsky's major works, key texts of the theosophical movement, are *Isis Unveiled* (1877) and *The Secret Doctrine* (1888).

the more familiar figures of Christian tradition: Michael had originally been Wotan; Peter, Donar; and so on. There were even odder attempts to distinguish ancient pagan traces. Von List advanced the theory that the heraldic devices of the Austrian aristocracy were disguised runic figures, and produced copious and elaborate examples (Goodrick-Clarke 1985, 71, especially plate 7); Philipp Stauff thought he could make out runic shapes in the complex patterns of half-timbered houses (Goodrick-Clarke 1985, 132). Even medieval architecture was supposed to encode ancient wisdom in its decorative stonemasonry. This longing to see behind and beyond the material world, to share in ancient wisdom kept secret from the common herd, has always proved tempting, and will no doubt continue to do so, as the success of Dan Brown's novel *The Da Vinci Code* readily illustrates. The tendency to read verbal messages in abstract patterns is a diagnostic symptom of a form of dementia known as Lewy Body disease.

Von List's contribution to theories of runic magic came when, in 1902, after a distinctly Odinic period of blindness following a cataract operation, he had a sudden major insight into a fundamental connexion between runes and magic. Pondering the verses in *Hávamál* concerning Óðinn's taking up of the runes, von List identified the eighteen spells of which the speaker claims knowledge with what he himself regarded as the original and ideal form of the runic *futhark*, or runic alphabet, which had eighteen characters. Thus, von List reasoned, each individual runic letter carried its own runic spell, its own magical charge—just as Sir William Temple had speculated, over three centuries earlier (Seaton 1935, 230).

It would be a mistake to overlook the serious ideological underpinning and, indeed, entailment, of these apparently foolish ideas. Von List's dismissal of Christianity was fuelled not only by a sort of misguided patriotism, but also by the pervasive anti-semitic conviction that Christianity was fatally compromised by its Jewish roots. His celebration of the superior Aryan 'racial' origins of the Germanic nation was both ominous and influential in obvious and, with hindsight, predictable, ways. And von List drew on Tacitus's ethnography of the Germanic tribes to invent the *Armanenschaft*, a sort of ruling political priesthood, initiated into the sacred mysteries of ariosophy, and ready to establish a social order in Germany in which Tacitus's three Germanic tribes are recast as three estates (the name *Armanenschaft* is derived from Tacitus's old name for the Germanic people, the Hermiones). This new political order would be characterized by patriarchy, racial purity, rule by a secret élite, and strong leadership. With the help of this strong leadership, a new world order would be founded in Germany, thereby fulfilling the occult prophecies of Madame Blavatsky and her followers. Von List's belief in this vision was confirmed by a verse from *Vǫluspá* (Dronke 1997, 87):

> Þá kemr hinn ríki
> at regindómi,
> ǫflugr, ofan,
> sá er ǫllu ræðr.

> Then comes the Mighty One
> to divine judgement;
> powerful, [he comes] from above,
> he who rules all things

Von List translated this descending power as 'Ein Stärke von Oben' ('a strong one from above') and the imaginary figure became a key element in his and his followers' predictions for Germany's glorious future (Goodrick-Clarke 1985, 88). It is ironic, then, that Dronke has dismissed the stanza as a Christian insertion, not part of the original poem (Dronke 1997, 87).

With a specificity which is chilling to look back on, von List's ideological package even included German union with Austria. Goodrick-Clarke has shown how such ideas fed, both directly and indirectly, into Nazi ideology, though von List's pseudo-historical occultism was not given much official credit: Hitler himself dismissed Wotanists—those who claimed to have resurrected the original pagan religion of the Germanic people—and proponents of *völkisch* ideas out of hand (Goodrick-Clarke 1985, 200–02).

But if runic magic and Wotanism were disparaged by the Nazi leadership, the runic alphabet continued to carry associations of German nationalism, Aryan racism, and the political and social order which was supposed, triumphantly, to be at hand. German runologists declared (without the very least foundation for it, beyond discerning its shape in Egyptian pyramids) that the **H** rune—*hagall*—was the most powerful, and had first been spun to whisk the whole universe into being; its name was used as the title of an influential National Socialist journal (Goodrick-Clarke 1985, 158), and it is currently the name of a white supremacist website.[8] Heinrich Himmler engaged a leading mystic nationalist, Karl Maria Wiligut, to design the iconography of the SS; in

---

[8] <http://www.nationalvanguard.org/story.php?id=8122>

this way came into being the distinctive double **S** rune as part of the uniform.[9] And research into Old Norse mythology, literature, and history was used as a cover for racist, proto-Nazi societies such as the Thule Society, or the Listian Edda Society.[10]

The founder of the Edda Society was Rudolf John Gorsleben, who believed that the *Edda* itself was an incomparably valuable source of Aryan wisdom. His thought was basically Listian, and he believed that the 'zenith of power' of the Aryan race was to be 'remanifested through a combination of eugenics and the systematic reawakening of occult powers and abilities' (Thorsson 1989, 15–17). In other words, he insisted that all racially pure Aryan individuals were united not only by their (superior) racial identity, but also by their privileged ability to re-connect with the driving force of the universe itself. The instruments of this connexion were runes. Runes had magical properties; as Goodrick-Clarke puts it, Gorsleben 'regarded runes as conductors of a subtle energy that animated the entire universe, and therefore as devices which could be used to influence the material world and the course of events' (Goodrick-Clarke 1985, 157). But more mystically, runes were a vital conduit between the Aryan god and Aryan man. The declared aim of the Edda Society was 'to conduct research into the ancient Aryan religion through the interpretation, via the runes, of Norse mythology'. But in 1933, the society's own journal, *Hag All All Hag* published an article which formally linked the society's aims and ideals with those of National Socialism. One wonders how welcome that was to the Nazi party.

Of course, the 'subtle energy that animated the entire universe' was not a mere fantasy on Gorsleben's part. Throughout the latter part of the nineteenth century and the first half of the twentieth, scientists were making extraordinary advances in the discovery and technology of all kinds of invisible radiation—radioactivity, X-rays, the electromagnetic radiation of radio waves, and so on. In 1936, Victor Hess (himself an Austrian, as it happened) was awarded the Nobel Prize for the discovery of cosmic rays, which he described as a powerful radiation which penetrates the universe from Outer Space. Any mystic with even the slightest tendency to paranoia would be thrilled and horrified. Gorsleben's twist on all this new and exciting science was that runes could be used to

---

[9] For an indefensibly sympathetic account of Wiligut's career and beliefs, see Flowers [Edred Thorsson] and Moynihan 2001.

[10] See Kavenna 2005 for an account of the Thule Society.

channel and harness these powerful sources of energy, like lightning conductors, or radio antennae.

This brings us at last to Marby and his runic gymnastics. Like Gorsleben, Marby too saw the world as infused with an invisible, quasi-divine, energy. But he developed the theory that runic characters were a schematic illustration of the various bodily postures which devotees might adopt in order to channel this cosmic energy (Goodrick-Clarke 1985, 160–61). Marby's aim was not primarily to establish a mystical connexion between Aryan man and Aryan god, but to draw down into individuals the supposedly health-giving and healing properties of the invisible energy. Runic gymnastics was basically a form of revitalizing yoga. In fact, one of Marby's followers, Siegfried Kummer, developed a set of techniques which he called *Runenyoga* (runic yoga) and he too was denounced for 'bringing the Holy Aryan heritage into disrepute and ridicule' (Goodrick-Clarke 1985, 162).

Runic gymnastics, or runic yoga, is easier to illustrate than to describe. It is not difficult to arrange the human body in ways which mimic quite closely many of the shapes of runic characters, although some postures are evidently more challenging than others. As far as one can see from Kummer's own illustrations of the various postures, the (inauthentic) **Z** rune needs an imaginary bolt of energy through the body to represent the cross bar, and it is clear that the shapes of some characters have been modified to fit the gymnastic scheme.[11] Current online instructions to would-be gymnasts note that Marby himself, in line with what little is known of pre-Christian worship from early texts, claimed that energy levels were highest if the performance took place out of doors. It is recommended that ideally practitioners should be naked, aligned with the earth's magnetic field, and prepared to wait patiently for the vibrations which signal the currents of energy. The perhaps unexpected side-effects of runic gymnastics are carefully set out: twitching, cramps, and energy thrusts are healthy, as are yawning, warm sweating, and increased bowel function. But a cold sweat is a dangerous symptom: the gymnast is warned to release the posture immediately.[12]

There were to be many other variations on rune gymnastics: rune yodelling, rune humming, making runic shapes with fingers, and so on.

---

[11] Most easily available online, at <http://www.geocities.com/odinistlibrary/OLArticles/Articles/karlspiesberger.htm>.

[12] <http://www.kondor.de/runes/runengymnastik.html>. See also Thorsson 1989, especially ch. 7.

According to Thorsson, for instance, Alpine 'yodling' [sic] represents 'ancient sacred mantric formulas', and he claims that the strings of runic letters which make up some unintelligible runic inscriptions are actually the notation of such protracted vocal formulas.[13] Rune humming, promoted by both Marby and Kummer, involves vocalizing the supposed phonetic value of the runic characters (obviously, one can hum vowels and nasal consonants, but plosives have to be systematically stuttered, as 'KA KE KI KO KU') (Thorsson 1989, 63). And the cult continues: in 1958, for example, Karl Spiesberger published *Runenexerzitien für Jederman* ('Runic Exercises for Everyman'). A current website advertising the book describes Spiesberger as 'an initiate of the magical order known as the "Fraternis Saturni" or "Brotherhood of Saturn". This magical lodge was/is [. . .] the most prestigious, prominent and magical order of German occultism' (see note 11). Thorsson offers instructions for making runic hand shapes based on Spiesberger's theories: for instance, one element in a 'rite of success' is prescribed as follows (Thorsson 1989, 76):

> Next form the hand posture of the **S**-rune in front of the body at about eye level. When this is done, dynamically say, 'The might in me is victorious!' When this is said, you should feel an oscillation of power between the heart center and the **S**-rune formed by the hands.

No doubt this requires a degree of practice. Thorsson's instructions and illustrations for 'Group Rune Rituals' are very diverting (Thorsson 1989, 97–104).

Some contemporary practitioners of rune magic clearly echo the racist ideology of figures such as von List and Gorsleben; for them, runic magic is inextricably bound up with German nationalism and mystic racism, a way of tapping into what they celebrate as the ancient Aryan 'race-soul' of the Nordic people. It is sometimes (but not always) symptomatic of racist sites and publications that the runic alphabet in question is based on the 'Armanic system' of eighteen runic characters. The use of this, rather than a twenty-four-character *futhark*, betrays its basis in Listian racist ideology, since it was von List who advanced the connexion between the ancient Germanic *Armanen*—the priestly élite whose name is taken from Tacitus's tribe of Hermiones— and the occult wisdom associated with Óðinn and his eighteen spells. But as a trawl through the very many websites on runes will show,

---

[13] Thorsson 1989, 89–90. The point is illustrated by representations of such 'calls' in musical notation.

the majority of practitioners pursue a gentler, New-Age runic magic, largely for telling fortunes. This most often involves the association of each runic character, without obvious justification, with individual items from apparently limitlessly various categories—genders, colours, times of day, kinds of weather, seasons, trees, herbs, elements, semi-precious stones, emotions, diseases, and so on. In this way, each rune is the supposed harbinger or predictor of a constellation of ailments, lucky numbers, charms, personality traits, or favourable life-style choices. A very contemporary twist is the association of each runic character with a particular essential oil (Pennick 1998, 159). Any number of websites will offer you a reading of your runes, for a very modest charge.

There is a postscript to the story of Friedrich Bernhard Marby and the Nazi administration which imprisoned him in Dachau until it was liberated by the Allied Forces in 1945. Karl Maria Wiligut, to whom Himmler had entrusted the iconography of the SS uniform, was a fanatical ariosophist, convinced that his own family was descended from an ancient royal Germanic master race whose religion—Irminism—had caused them to be persecuted not only by the Christian church, but also by Jews and Freemasons. Irminists regarded 'Baldur-Chrestos' as their prophet, murdered by Wotanists in 9600 BC.[14] Wiligut wrote about runes and Norse myths under the pseudonym 'Jarl Vidar' (in Norse myth, Víðarr was the son of Óðinn, who at Ragnarǫk executed magnificent revenge for the death of his father by tearing apart the jaws of the monstrous wolf Fenrir). Wiligut (having changed his name to Weisthor) helped to create 'pagan wedding ceremonies for SS officers and their brides, at which [he] officiated with an ivory-handled stick [. . .] carved with runes' (Goodrick-Clarke 1985, 187). And this was the man who charged Kummer and Marby with 'bringing the Holy Aryan heritage into disrepute'. The dividing line between Nordic revivalism such as Wiligut's, which the Nazis seemed to find acceptable, and what they regarded as its unacceptable face—runic gymnastics—is not a self-evident one to modern commentators.

---

[14] For a full account of Wiligut/Weisthor's activities, see Goodrick-Clarke 1985, ch 14. Flowers and Moynihan 2001 contains translations of Wiligut's mystical writings. Flowers's introduction implies that Wiligut's incarceration for insanity was unjust; a glance at these writings suggests quite the opposite.

Bibliography

Baker, Alan 2000. *Invisible Eagle: The Hidden History of Nazi Occultism.*
Bjarni Einarsson 1975. *Litterære forudsætninger for Egils saga.*
Blavatsky, Helena Petrovna 1877. *Isis Unveiled: A Master-Key to the Mysteries of Ancient and Modern Science and Theology.* 2 vols.
Blavatsky, Helena 1888. *The Secret Doctrine: The Synthesis of Science, Religion, and Philosophy.* 2 vols.
Brate, Erik 1928. *Sveriges Runinskrifter.*
Breuilly, John, ed., 1992. *The State of Germany: The National Idea in the Making, Unmaking and Remaking of a Modern Nation-state.*
Dronke, Ursula, ed., 1997. *The Poetic Edda*: Vol. II. *The Mythological Poems.*
Evans, D. A. H., ed., 1986. *Hávamál.*
Faulkes, Anthony, ed., 1977. *Two Versions of Snorra Edda from the 17th Century.* Vol. II.
Flowers, Stephen E. [Edred Thorsson], trans., and Michael Moynihan, ed., 2001. *The Secret King: Karl Maria Wiligut, Himmler's Lord of the Runes.*
Geary, Patrick 2002. *The Myth of Nations: The Medieval Origins of Europe.*
Goodrick-Clarke, Nicholas 1985. *The Occult Roots of Nazism: The Ariosophists of Austria and Germany, 1890–1935.*
Guðni Jónsson, ed., 1936. *Grettis saga Ásmundarsonar.* Íslenzk fornrit VII.
Heaney, Seamus 1975. *North.*
Hutton, M. 1970. *Germania*, rev. E. H. Warmington. *Tacitus in Five Volumes.* vol. I.
Kavenna, Joanna 2005. *The Ice Museum: In Search of the Lost Land of Thule.*
Liestøl, Aslak 1968. 'Correspondence in Runes'. *Mediaeval Scandinavia* 1, 17–27.
Liestøl, Aslak 1974. 'Runic Voices from Towns of Ancient Norway'. *Scandinavica* 13, 19–33.
Magnus, Johannes 1554. *Historia [. . .] de omnibus Gothorum Sveonumque regibus.*
Malm, Mats 1994. 'Olaus Rudbeck's *Atlantis* and Old Norse Poetics'. In *Northern Antiquity: The Post-Medieval Reception of Edda and Saga.* Ed. Andrew Wawn, 1–25.
McKinnell, John and Rudolf Simek with Klaus Düwel 2004. *Runes, Magic and Religion: A Sourcebook.*
Neckel, Gustav, ed., 1962. *Edda. Die Lieder des Codex Regius nebst verwandten Denkmälern.* 4th edn, rev. Hans Kuhn.
Nordal, Sigurður, ed., 1933. *Egils saga Skalla-Grímssonar.* Íslenzk fornrit II.
Page, R. I. 1998. *The Icelandic Rune-poem.*
Pennick, Nigel 1998. *Secrets of the Runes: Discover the Magic of the Ancient Runic Alphabet.*
Quinn, Judy and Margaret Clunies Ross 1994. 'The Image of Norse Poetry and Myth in Seventeenth-Century England'. In *Northern Antiquity: The Post-Medieval Reception of Edda and Saga.* Ed. Andrew Wawn, 189–210.
Resen, Peder Hansen 1665. *Edda Islandorum.*
Roberts, Michael 1979. *The Swedish Imperial Experience, 1560–1718.*

Sawyer, Birgit 2000. *The Viking-Age Rune-Stones: Custom and Commemoration in Early Medieval Scandinavia.*

Scales, Len and Oliver Zimmer, eds, 2005. *Power and the Nation in European History.*

Seaton, Ethel 1935. *Literary Relations of England and Scandinavia in the Seventeenth Century.*

Spiesberger, Karl 1958. *Runenexerzitien für Jederman.*

Swanton, Michael, ed., 1970. *The Dream of the Rood.*

Thorsson, Edred 1989. *Rune Might: Secret Practices of the German Rune Magicians.*

White, Carolinne 1998. *Early Christian Lives.*

Worm, Ole 1636. *Antiquitates Danicæ; seu Literatura Runica.*

A VIKING PACIFIST? THE LIFE OF ST MAGNUS IN SAGA, NOVEL, AND OPERA

CARL PHELPSTEAD

The composer Peter Maxwell Davies begins a synopsis of his opera *The Martyrdom of St Magnus* with the remarkable assertion that 'St Magnus [. . .] is the Patron Saint of Orkney. He was a Viking pacifist' (Davies 1977, 7).[1] Davies goes on to state that 'The history of St Magnus is to be read in the Icelandic *Orkneyinga saga*', but a reader of that saga might question Davies's characterization of Magnus as a 'Viking pacifist'. This essay explores the transformations St Magnus underwent as the story of his life in *Orkneyinga saga* was retold in the twentieth century in the novel *Magnus* by the leading Orcadian writer George Mackay Brown (1921–1996), and then in the opera based on that novel by the eminent British composer, Peter Maxwell Davies (b. 1934).[2] For these two twentieth-century artists the Norse earl St Magnus is central to a sense of a peculiarly Orcadian identity, yet they also present him as a figure of wider resonance, a particular victim of violence who can stand for all those killed for their beliefs or their desire to make peace. Magnus is universalized in these twentieth-century reworkings by means of typological connections with other victims of violence. In this way, I shall argue, Brown and Davies adopt a more 'hagiographical' approach to their saintly subject than does the writer of *Orkneyinga saga*: they turn Magnus into a more straightforwardly exemplary, and so less complex, character than he is in the saga.

From the second half of the ninth century onwards the islands of Orkney and Shetland formed an earldom owing allegiance to the Norwegian king. The islands passed to Denmark with the union of the Danish and Norwegian crowns in 1380, and did not come under Scottish

---

[1] The synopsis is printed in the libretto (Davies 1977, 7–9) and the booklet to the CD recording of the opera (Davies 1990, 7–8).

[2] Brown and Davies used the translation of *Orkneyinga saga* by Taylor (1938). Since differences between this translation and the Norse text of *Orkneyinga saga* as edited in Finnbogi Guðmundsson 1965 do not significantly affect the argument of this essay, the saga is here quoted in Taylor's translation and I follow Taylor, Brown, and Davies in using anglicized spellings of Norse names: e.g. Magnus for Magnús, Hakon for Hákon, Paul for Páll.

rule until 1468–69, when the Danish king proved unable to pay a dowry he had secured on the islands. This Norse cultural inheritance has been, and still is, fundamental to the regional identity of Orkney and Shetland. A dialect of Norse, known as Norn, survived in the islands until as late as the eighteenth century, and the English of the islands still retains a high percentage of Norse loanwords (Marwick 1929, Barnes 1998). Sir Walter Scott emphasized the Norse identity of Shetland in his historical novel *The Pirate* (published in 1822), and several modern Orcadian writers have drawn on Viking history and Norse literature in their novels, poetry, and drama (see Scott 1996, D'Arcy 1996, chs 10–12). Orcadians and Shetlanders living in London in 1892 founded what is now the Viking Society for Northern Research, the publisher of this volume of essays and sponsor of the conferences at which they were presented (on the history of the Viking Society see Townsend 1992).

Vikings settled in, and ruled, many parts of the British Isles and Ireland, but of these areas only the Norse earldom of Orkney has a whole Icelandic saga devoted to its early history. This text, *Orkneyinga saga*, is the major surviving account of the history of Orkney between the ninth and the late twelfth century. The saga was probably put together with some input from Orcadian informants, and it incorporates a considerable amount of skaldic verse composed in Orkney or by Orcadians. The saga was compiled *c.*1200, but survives in a revised version made *c.*1230 and preserved in the late fourteenth-century Icelandic manuscript, Flateyjarbók (MS GKS 1005 fol.).[3]

A large proportion of *Orkneyinga saga* (chapters 34–52 and 57) is devoted to the life of Magnus Erlendson. His father and uncle were joint earls of Orkney; the territory was often divided between two or three rulers and the earldom suffered from recurrent conflicts between rival earls, as happened during the reigns of Magnus's father and uncle, and later when Magnus and his cousin, Hakon Paulson, were joint rulers of Orkney. It was Hakon's determination to be sole ruler of the earldom that drove him to have Magnus executed on 16 April 1117. Magnus was soon regarded as a Christian martyr and saint, someone to whom one could pray for miraculous assistance. Magnus's nephew, Earl (later St) Rognvaldr Kali Kol's son (d. 1158/59), played a major role in the development of Magnus's cult and began the construction of St Magnus Cathedral in Kirkwall in 1137.

[3] On the manuscripts, date, and sources of *Orkneyinga saga* see Finnbogi Guðmundsson 1965, v–lxxxi, cviii–cxxvi.

Saga

The account of St Magnus in *Orkneyinga saga* is almost certainly based on a Latin saint's life, which no longer survives in its original form, but which is known to scholars as **Vita sancti Magni*, and which may have been composed in 1137 (for a recent examination of the dating and authorship of the *Vita* see Haki Antonsson 2004, especially 44–47 and 61–63). Besides the account in *Orkneyinga saga* there are also two other biographies of St Magnus in Old Norse: *Magnúss saga skemmri* (The Shorter Saga of Magnus), from the mid-thirteenth century, and *Magnúss saga lengri* (The Longer Saga of Magnus), from the fourteenth. Both of these later sagas are based on *Orkneyinga saga,* but *Magnúss saga lengri* also includes several extensive passages, mainly of a homiletic rather than narrative nature, translated directly from the lost Latin **Vita sancti Magni* (on these texts see Finnbogi Guðmundsson 1965, cxxviii–cxxxviii).

The Earl Magnus portrayed in the Old Norse sources is a more complex character than is usually found in medieval hagiography. Early in *Orkneyinga saga*'s account of his reign (chapter 45) there is an idealized description of Magnus as a model ruler which includes some remarks on his attitude to Vikings: he was

> hard and unsparing towards robbers and vikings. He put to death many men who plundered the bonder and common people. He had murderers and thieves seized, and punished rich as well as poor for robbery and theft and all misdeeds. (Taylor 1938, 205)

In the next chapter, however, the narrator says of Hakon and Magnus that

> it is said in the poem on the subject, that they fought with the chief called Donald [. . .] who was the second cousin to the Earls; and he fell before them. There was a man of rank called Thorbjorn whom they put to death in Burra Firth in Shetland. [And it is said that they took the house over his head and burned him in it] (Taylor 1938, 205–06).

The poem referred to here no longer survives, but as Thomson says, 'The poem, although lost, provides enough evidence to dispose of Magnus-the-pacifist' (Thomson 2003, 52). The sentence Taylor places in brackets at the end of the above quotation is found in a sixteenth-century Danish translation of *Orkneyinga saga* and in *Magnúss saga skemmri*, but not in the Flateyjarbók text of *Orkneyinga saga*: it is likely that at some point in the textual tradition a scribe deleted this sentence, recognizing that saints ought not to burn people in their homes. These passages reveal an ideal of the Christian ruler far removed from the kind of pacifist

Brown and Davies later portray; moreover, the killing of his second cousin, Duncan, and the burning of Thorbjorn suggest that some of Magnus's deeds were of a very dubious moral quality.

The description of Earl Magnus in chapter 45 continues with an account of his ten years of chaste marriage to an aristocratic Scottish woman:

> He consorted with her ten years in such wise that he fulfilled the lusts of neither of them and was pure and clean from all carnal sins. And if he felt temptation coming over him, he bathed in cold water and prayed for the intercession of God. (Taylor 1938, 205)

This account of Magnus's sexual abstinence needs to be seen in the context both of hagiographic commonplaces (for example, the motif of immersion in water as a prophylactic for sin (Ireland 1997)) and of the history of the institution of 'spiritual marriage' (see Elliott 1993; McGlynn and Moll 1996). Dyan Elliott shows that in this period it was usual for the wife rather than the husband to initiate a commitment to a chaste or 'spiritual' marriage and she suggests that in this context Magnus's taking of the initiative associates his commitment to chastity with remorse over a youth misspent as a Viking (Elliott 1993, 247). This is not, however, a connection that is made explicitly by the medieval writers.

The incident which, more than any other, lies behind Peter Maxwell Davies's characterization of Magnus as a 'Viking pacifist' occurs earlier in the saga, before Magnus has become an earl. Magnus is forced by his namesake King Magnus Bare-legs of Norway to accompany him on a military expedition to the Hebrides and then on to Wales. While on this expedition the Norwegian forces engage with those of two Welsh earls in the Menai Strait. As the other men prepare to fight, Magnus sits down on deck and refuses to arm himself: he says that he has no quarrel with anyone there, and 'therefore I will not fight' (Taylor 1938, 199). Instead of fighting, Magnus 'took a Psalter and sang through the fighting but did not go into shelter' (Taylor 1938, 199). Given what George Mackay Brown and Peter Maxwell Davies do with this passage, it is worth drawing attention to the king's statement that 'I do not think that religious belief is at the bottom of this' (Taylor 1938, 199): this comment hints at other possible motivations for Magnus's behaviour that are ignored by Brown and Davies (King Magnus had earlier deprived his namesake's father and uncle of the earldom of Orkney). The saga emphasizes that the battle is long and hard, but Magnus miraculously remains unharmed. No doubt it is Magnus's behaviour in this battle which prompted Davies to describe him as a 'Viking pacifist', but Peter Foote (1988, 200–02) has pointed out that unlike other soldier-saints, such as St Martin, who permanently renounce violence, Magnus is not actually a pacifist, but rather a proponent of 'Just War' theory: at this point he refuses to fight not because he is against all fighting, but only because he does not have a just cause against the Welsh ('He said he had no quarrel with any man there' (Taylor 1938, 199)).

Magnus escapes after the Battle of Anglesey and does not return to Orkney until after King Magnus and Earls Paul and Erlend have died, when his cousin Hakon Paulson is persuaded to allow Magnus to reign with him as joint earl. Some years later, however, Hakon tricks Magnus into attending a peace meeting on the island of Egilsay. Although Magnus's subsequent 'martyrdom' is solely a result of Hakon's political ambitions, the accounts of it are influenced by the biblical narratives of Christ's Passion and by hagiographic conventions: Magnus's spending the night praying in a church after arriving on Egilsay, for example, echoes Christ's watching in the Garden of Gethsemane on the night of His arrest (Taylor 1938, 208 cf. Matthew 26: 36–46 and parallels).

Magnus faces death as befits a Christian martyr, 'blithe as if he had been bidden to a feast' (Taylor 1938, 210). He prays for his enemies and then asks his executioner to strike him on the head rather than behead him: 'for it is not seemly to behead chiefs like thieves. [. . .] After that he crossed himself, and bowed himself to the stroke' (Taylor 1938, 211).

Magnus's first posthumous miracle is recorded in the next chapter: after his death the place of his martyrdom becomes a green field (Taylor 1938, 211). Further miracles are reported in chapter 52, including the appearance of a heavenly light over the grave, and chapter 57 of *Orkneyinga saga* comprises a collection of very brief accounts of Magnus's miracles, mostly healings, which further emphasizes the popular nature of the saint's cult.

There can be no doubt that the writer of *Orkneyinga saga* believed Magnus to be a saint, but this does not prevent him hinting at less than saintly motives for some of Magnus's actions, nor lead him to shrink from recounting deeds, such as the slaying of Magnus's second cousin, Donald, and the burning of Thorbjorn, which are less than wholly edifying.

Novel

George Mackay Brown was born in Orkney and, apart from a few years as a student at the University of Edinburgh, he lived there for the whole of his life. Much of his writing is inspired by the history of Orkney, and informed by his sense of the Norse cultural inheritance of the islands, but he never learned Old Norse, claiming not to have been able to afford the textbook for the Old Norse course at Edinburgh University (D'Arcy 1996, 282 n. 39). Dependent therefore on translations, Brown used the version of *Orkneyinga saga* produced by A. B. Taylor in 1938; when Hermann Pálsson and Paul Edwards later published their translation they dedicated it to Brown (Hermann Pálsson and Edwards 1981, 5).

References to the life and death of St Magnus can be found in writings produced throughout George Mackay Brown's career, with extended treatments in *An Orkney Tapestry* (Brown 1973, first published 1969), *The Loom of Light* (1984), *Songs for St Magnus Day* (1988), and the novel *Magnus* (Brown 1988, first published 1973). Brown became a Roman Catholic in 1961, and his reworkings of material from *Orkneyinga saga* are deeply influenced by Christian pacifist beliefs. This influence is clearly seen, for example, when he refers in *An Orkney Tapestry* to Magnus's words before the Battle of the Menai Strait:

> 'I have no quarrel with any man here' —it was the first time in the recorded history of the north that that remark had been made. [. . .] Some day soon all men everywhere will have to speak it, if the nations are not to be involved in a final holocaust; and after that, perhaps, the saints will inherit the earth. (Brown 1973, 74)

In *An Orkney Tapestry* Magnus's martyrdom is represented as the turning point in Orcadian history, the moment when the inadequate ethics of the pre-Christian period (with which Magnus's opponent Hakon is associated) begin to be superseded by a new Christian ethic. In this text Brown remains close to his source material in *Orkneyinga saga*, including, for example, the information given in the saga about Magnus and Hakon killing their own second cousin and burning another chieftain inside his house (Brown 1973, 78). In his later, more extended, treatment in the novel *Magnus*, however, Brown omits material that reflects poorly on the eponymous saint and makes some significant alterations to other aspects of the historical narrative provided by *Orkneyinga saga*.

Julian D'Arcy, who has written most illuminatingly on Brown's use of Old Norse sources, notes three specific changes of historical fact which Brown makes in *Magnus* (D'Arcy 1996, 267–69).[4] First, whereas

[4] Studies of the novel preceding D'Arcy 1996 include Huberman 1981, Rowena Murray 1986, and D'Arcy 1994; the later reprint of *Magnus* includes an introduction by Isobel Murray (1998). Thomson's recent brief remarks on the novel's relationship to its saga sources adumbrate a reading along lines similar to those developed in the present essay (cf. Thomson 2003, 43, 52, 54, 61–62).

Orkneyinga saga says that King Magnus Bare-legs deposed Magnus's father and uncle, Earls Erlend and Paul, Brown claims the exact opposite, that the king confirmed them as rulers in Orkney (Brown 1998, 54–55). This removes the possibility of interpreting St Magnus's refusal to fight in the Menai Strait as merely a protest against the king's having deprived his family of power. Second, Brown stresses that Orkney had been torn apart by civil strife for centuries before Magnus's martyrdom: D'Arcy points out that this is an exaggeration, but Brown's suggestion that Magnus's death brought to an end a long-running and bitter civil war, rather than merely averting one, invests that death with greater significance and emphasizes the value and efficacy of pacifism as a means of ending bloodshed. Third, in *Orkneyinga saga* Magnus offers his cousin alternatives that would not require him to order Magnus's execution, but in the novel these suggestions are made by others while Magnus is absent: in this way Brown removes any hint that the saint had an interest in preserving his own life.

Brown's novel *Magnus* also includes new material which is designed to enhance the image of Magnus as a perfectly exemplary figure. In chapter 2 the young Magnus shows his concern for suffering creatures by caring for a wounded seal; he renounces the worldly values of his contemporaries by refusing to use his own name:

> I do not like my name. It means 'great, powerful'. I don't want to be great and powerful. The world is sick because of people wanting to be great and powerful. (Brown 1998, 38).

As in the medieval sources, Magnus spends the Battle of the Menai Strait singing from a Psalter, but the novel does not comment on Magnus's reasons for refusing to fight: whereas in *Orkneyinga saga* Magnus states quite clearly that he will not fight because he has no quarrel with the Welsh, the lack of such an explanation in Brown's account implies that Magnus is a pacifist opposed to all violence on principle.

In chapter 4 of the novel, 'The Temptations', Magnus is seen grappling with, and ultimately resisting sexual temptation, the temptation to deprive Hakon of his share of the earldom, and the temptation to retire to a monastery and so refuse the responsibilities put upon him by God. Brown's handling of Magnus's chaste marriage displays a touching sympathy for Ingerth, the earl's wife—much more sympathy than the medieval saga-writers showed (Brown 1998, 61–65).

The most remarkable innovation in Brown's *Magnus* occurs in chapter 7, 'The Killing'. The peace meeting between Magnus and Hakon on the island of Egilsay is here relocated to the twentieth century, so that the narrative suddenly leaps forwards eight centuries. Journalists interview witnesses of the events, and the execution scene takes place in a Nazi concentration camp: the camp's commanders force Lifolf, the camp's cook and butcher, to kill Magnus, and the execution is described from the perspective of this unwilling participant. Magnus himself is described as 'the Lutheran pastor whose books were burned at the start of the war' (1998, 167). This statement, together with the fact that in the novel Magnus is hanged rather than struck on the head as in *Orkneyinga saga*, clearly identifies Magnus with the German Protestant churchman and martyr Dietrich Bonhoeffer, who was hanged in the Flossenburg concentration camp on 9 April 1945 for his involvement in a conspiracy to assassinate Hitler.

By conflating St Magnus and Dietrich Bonhoeffer in this way, Brown identifies both men as manifestations of a trans-historical type of the Christian martyr: as in medieval hagiography, the attributes of the universal type become more important than the historical individuality of each particular martyr; what matters is the way they are assimilated to a pattern, a paradigm that connects the saint's life with the lives of other saints and of Christ. Medieval hagiographers defended such a procedure on theological grounds. Gregory of Tours, for example, wrote in the Preface to his *Liber vitae patrum*:

> Et quaeritur a quibusdam, utram vita[m] sanctorum an vitas dicere debeamus. [. . .] manifestum est, melius dici vitam patrum quam vitas, quia, cum sit diversitas meritorum virtutumque, una tamen omnes vita corpores alit in mundo. (quoted in Heffernan 1988, 7)

> And it will be asked by some whether we ought to speak of the life or the lives of the saints. [. . .] It is clear that it is better to say life rather than lives of the fathers because, although there is a diversity of merit and virtue, in this world one life nourishes all their bodies.

It did not even matter if a particular story was told about the wrong saint, provided that the story was edifying. Reginald of Canterbury admits in the Preface to his *Life of St Malchus* that if he came across a good story anywhere he included it on the grounds that all things are common in the communion of saints (Jones 1947, 61).

Isobel Murray points out that in identifying Magnus with the Protestant Bonhoeffer 'Brown's analysis of suffering, virtue and sacrifice is not confined to canonised, Catholic saints' (1998, x). The narrator of *Magnus* meditates at length on the nature of sacrifice in the chapter on the killing of St Magnus, and in doing so ranges widely beyond Christian martyrdom to consider the meanings of prehistoric sacrifices in

Orkney and human sacrifices among the Aztecs of Central America (Brown 1998, ch. 7).

This meditation points to the importance of Christ's Crucifixion, the model for both Magnus and Bonhoeffer, and an event the novel's narrator describes as 'the one only central sacrifice of history' (1998, 158). Magnus hears Mass the day before his execution, and the narrator reflects on the Eucharistic sacrifice and that of St Magnus in a key passage that encapsulates the aesthetic informing both this novel and Davies's opera:

> All time was gathered up into that ritual half-hour, the entire history of mankind [...]. That is to say, history both repeats itself and does not repeat itself. One event; one group of characters that move in and through and out of the event, and both make the event and are changed by it, collectively and individually—that event bears resemblances to another event that occurred a hundred years before, so that a man listening to a saga is moved to say, 'This is the same performance all over again.' It is not: [...] Events are never the same, but they have enough similarity for one to say tentatively that there are constants in human nature, and constants in the human situation [...].
>
> Poetry, art, music thrive on these constants. They gather into themselves a huge scattered diversity of experience and reduce them to patterns. (Brown 1998, 129)

This justification for the typological identifications that Brown makes is comparable to the theological defence of similar procedures by Gregory of Tours and Reginald of Canterbury referred to above: both the medieval hagiographers and the modern novelist emphasize pattern over diversity.

Brown's additions and changes to *Orkneyinga saga* all seem to be made with the same purpose in mind: as D'Arcy puts it, 'to play down the fallible and human aspects of Magnus and to emphasise his saintliness' (D'Arcy 1996, 269). At the beginning of *An Orkney Tapestry* Brown refers to a distinction made by a fellow Orcadian, Edwin Muir, between Story, 'the facts of our history', and Fable, 'the vision by which people live' (Brown 1973, 1–2). Brown's versions of the life of St Magnus are clearly 'Fable' in Muir's sense, a 'vision by which people live': Brown invests the saga account with his own Christian pacifist vision and departs from his source in order to convey that vision the more effectively. There is, however, a danger that this strategy might back-fire, as D'Arcy suggests:

> the result may be a greater wariness and scepticism towards Mackay Brown's intentions, especially if these seem overtly didactic. In this sense, Mackay Brown's manipulation of the saga may have defeated his own ends. (D'Arcy 1996, 270)

Brown's departures from *Orkneyinga saga* may be justified in terms of turning History into Fable, but his adaptation of the story for ideological and didactic purposes contrasts strangely and ironically with his own lament in *An Orkney Tapestry* that 'We cannot get a clear picture of the man [Magnus] because his monkish biographer has smudged the outline with conventional pious platitudes' (1973, 71).

Opera

Brown's simplification of *Orkneyinga saga*'s portrait of St Magnus is carried even further by Peter Maxwell Davies in his opera, *The Martyrdom of St Magnus*, which sets the composer's own libretto based on Brown's *Magnus*. Davies was born in Salford in 1934, but visited Orkney in 1970 and has lived there since 1974 (Griffiths 1985, 20; Seabrook 1994, 124, 144). Davies enjoyed a long and productive association with Brown, setting several of his poems to music and basing other works on Brown's fiction. *The Martyrdom of St Magnus* was commissioned by the BBC in celebration of the Queen's Silver Jubilee and was first performed on 18 June 1977 at the opening of the first St Magnus Festival in Kirkwall, Orkney.[5] The piece is called 'A Chamber Opera in nine scenes', and deploys modest forces of just five singers (who sing twenty-six roles!) and eleven instrumentalists (flute, clarinet, horn, trumpets, percussion, guitar, keyboards, and strings). In its ritualistic form, and to some extent musically, the piece is highly reminiscent of Benjamin Britten's Church Parables. As in many of Davies's other compositions, a major influence on the music is Gregorian chant, an influence which is here justified in terms of Magnus's own familiarity with plainsong (Davies 1985, 163).[6]

Brown's *Magnus* is as much a meditation as a novel. But it also has obvious dramatic potential: some parts of the novel are arranged on the page as if they were part of a play, with the names of speakers printed before their parts of the dialogue and no intervening narrative prose; Murray (1998, ix) writes that the book is 'A series of tableaux, deliberately isolated from each other', and this tableaux structure transforms easily into the nine scenes of Davies's small-scale chamber opera.

[5] On the original production and subsequent tour taking in the Proms and several English cathedrals see Seabrook 1994, 165–66. The opera was also revived as part of a retrospective of the composer's work at the South Bank in 1990 (Seabrook 1994, 232).

[6] This composer's note on the opera is printed in Davies 1985, 162–63 and in the booklet accompanying the CD recording of the opera (Davies 1990, 4–5).

Davies openly acknowledges that his portrait lacks the paradoxical complexity of the saga accounts:

> Inevitably, there had to be simplification—Magnus, for instance, is not such a complex character in the opera as in the novel, and certainly not as multi-faceted as in John Mooney's study in depth. (Davies 1985, 162; the reference here is to the extensive study of the medieval accounts of St Magnus in Mooney 1935.)

In this passage there is both an implicit recognition that Brown's portrait is already a simplification of the complex character that Mooney found in the medieval sources, and also an open acknowledgement that the opera takes this process of simplification still further.

The first scene of the opera is 'The Battle of Menai Strait', in which a Welsh and a Norse herald converse, interrupted briefly by Magnus's singing from his Psalter. As in Brown's novel, Magnus offers no explanation for his refusal to fight and it is therefore logical to assume that he is a pacifist, with a hatred of all fighting. The scene which follows shows Magnus tempted to marry: whereas in *Orkneyinga saga* and the novel he enters into a chaste marriage, in the opera he refuses to marry at all; his bride to be then turns away and 'The reverse of her mask is seen to be a Beast' (1977, 16). In this way Davies shows Magnus dealing with sexual temptation in a way that no longer has to be interpreted in terms of the peculiarly medieval theological framework of the chaste marriage.

The most significant change, as opposed to simple omission, that Davies makes to Brown's novel occurs in Scenes VII and VIII, the representation of Magnus's martyrdom. Davies writes that

> The novel has Magnus martyred in a (Nazi) concentration camp; I decided to bring the martyrdom forward to the present, and set it in the country where the opera is performed—an attempt to make audiences aware of the possibilities with us for such a murder of a political or religious figure, whatever his convictions. (Davies 1985, 163)

In Scene VI of the opera Hakon rejects proposed alternatives to having Magnus murdered. Scene VII, 'The Reporters', then leaps forward nearly nine hundred years to show the modern mass media reporting on events on Egilsay as the peace meeting fails: reporters make brief reports and local residents provide interviews. This chronological disruption is accompanied musically by 'a brilliant series of pastiches' (Griffiths 1985, 94) culminating in a foxtrot, a dance that represents 'an image of total corruption' in Davies's musical language (Griffiths 1985, 67).

The setting of the following scene, 'The Sacrifice', is no longer tied to such a specific place and time as Brown's Nazi concentration camp, and the Military Officer's justification for the execution of Magnus—that 'The enemy we fear is the enemy within our borders'—can easily be read in contemporary terms by the opera's audience. As in Brown's novel, Magnus is hanged, rather than struck on the head as in the saga, and in so far as hanging is less obviously associated with particular places and periods than execution with a weapon, this small detail assists in universalizing Magnus's execution. The opera, like the novel, ends with the martyred Magnus miraculously granting sight to a blind beggar women called Mary. Blind Mary is granted not only sight, but also a spirit of prophecy, becoming what the libretto calls 'a Seer, a Prophetess'. Her words echo the meditation on sacrifice in chapter 7 of Brown's *Magnus* (Davies 1977, 31):

> Blind mouths, crying, still crying for sacrifice, for more sacrifice.
> There was one central sacrifice: 'I am the bread of Life.' [. . .]
> But men still crave sacrifice, so King Olaf died for you.
> So Earl Magnus died for you [. . .].
> And you shall know
> (*Pointing, seeing*)
> who else will die, who among you will be sacrificed, among the blind, hungry mouths;
> (*pointing*)
> who the victims, who the persecutors, the sacrificed, the slayer.

Mary's words link the sacrifices of Christ, the Norwegian royal protomartyr St Olaf (d. 1030), and St Magnus with possible, indeed inevitable, future sacrifices.[7]

Mary's pointing implicates members of the audience in these future sacrifices, whether as victims or as perpetrators, and Davies writes that his opera is 'an attempt to make audiences aware of the possibilities with us for such a murder of a political or religious figure, whatever his convictions' (Davies 1985, 163). Unlike Brown, the composer does not identify as a Christian, and the opera presents Magnus as perhaps even more widely representative than in the novel. By bringing Magnus's death fully up to date, the opera goes even further than the novel in claiming that there are what we have seen Brown (1998, 129) refer to as 'constants in human nature, and constants in the human situation'.

---

[7] In an interview Davies reveals that he was also thinking of St Thomas Becket during the composition of this scene (Griffiths 1985, 109), an interesting observation given the connections between the cults of Magnus and Thomas recently detailed by Haki Antonsson (2004).

That George Mackay Brown and Peter Maxwell Davies chose to retell the life of St Magnus of Orkney is easily explicable in terms of the saint's prominence in Orcadian cultural history, his status as the islands' patron saint, and his importance to an Orcadian sense of regional identity. Despite this intensely local interest, however, both the novelist and the composer find in the Icelandic *Orkneyinga saga* a figure of universal, not merely local, resonance, one in whose self-sacrificial acceptance of death a perpetually recurring pattern of human experience is made manifest.

Bibliography

Barnes, Michael 1998. *The Norn Language of Orkney and Shetland*.
Brown, George Mackay [1969] 1973. *An Orkney Tapestry*.
Brown, George Mackay 1984. *The Loom of Light*. In *Three Plays*.
Brown, George Mackay 1988. *Songs for St Magnus Day: The Seven Jars of Sorrow and Comfort*.
Brown, George Mackay [1973] 1998. *Magnus*.
D'Arcy, Julian Meldon 1994. 'George Mackay Brown and *Orkneyinga saga*'. In *Northern Antiquity: The Post-Medieval Reception of Edda and Saga*. Ed. Andrew Wawn, 305–27.
D'Arcy, Julian Meldon 1996. *Scottish Skalds and Sagamen: Old Norse Influence on Modern Scottish Literature*.
Davies, Peter Maxwell 1977. *The Martyrdom of St Magnus: A Chamber Opera in Nine Scenes: Libretto by the Composer after the Novel Magnus by George Mackay Brown*.
Davies, Peter Maxwell 1985. 'The Martyrdom of St. Magnus'. In Griffiths 1985, 162–63.
Davies, Peter Maxwell 1990. *The Martyrdom of St Magnus: A Chamber Opera in Nine Scenes*. Music Theatre Wales, Scottish Chamber Opera Ensemble. Conducted by Michael Rafferty. Unicorn-Kanchana DKP (CD) 9100.
Elliott, Dyan 1993. *Spiritual Marriage: Sexual Abstinence in Medieval Wedlock*.
Finnbogi Guðmundsson, ed., 1965. *Orkneyinga Saga*. Íslenzk fornrit 34.
Foote, Peter 1988. 'Observations on *Orkneyinga saga*'. In *St Magnus Cathedral and Orkney's Twelfth-Century Renaissance*. Ed. Barbara E. Crawford, 192–207.
Griffiths, Paul 1985. *Peter Maxwell Davies*.
Haki Antonsson 2004. 'Two Twelfth-Century Martyrs: St Thomas of Canterbury and St Magnús of Orkney'. In *Sagas, Saints and Settlements*. Ed. Gareth Williams and Paul Bibire, 41–64.
Heffernan, Thomas J. 1988. *Sacred Biography: Saints and Their Biographers in the Middle Ages*.
Hermann Pálsson and Paul Edwards, trans., [1978] 1981. *Orkneyinga Saga: The History of the Earls of Orkney*.
Huberman, Elizabeth 1981. 'George Mackay Brown's *Magnus*'. *Studies in Scottish Literature* 16, 122–34.

Ireland, Colin 1997. 'Penance and Prayer in Water: An Irish Practice in Northumbrian Hagiography'. *Cambrian Medieval Celtic Studies* 34, 51–66.
Jones, Charles W. 1947. *Saints' Lives and Chronicles in Early England.*
Magnúss saga lengri. In Finnbogi Guðmundsson, ed., 1965, 335–83.
Magnúss saga skemmri. In Finnbogi Guðmundsson, ed., 1965, 311–32.
Marwick, Hugh 1929. *The Orkney Norn.*
McGlynn, Margaret and Richard J. Moll 1996. 'Chaste Marriage in the Middle Ages: "It were to hire a greet merite"'. In *Handbook of Medieval Sexuality*. Ed. Vern L. Bullough and James A. Brundage, 103–22.
Mooney, John 1935. *St. Magnus—Earl of Orkney.*
Murray, Isobel 1998. 'Introduction'. In Brown 1998, vii–xi.
Murray, Rowena 1986. 'The Influence of Norse Literature on the Twentieth-century Writer George Mackay Brown'. In *Scottish Language and Literature, Medieval and Renaissance: Fourth International Conference 1984: Proceedings.* Ed. Dietrich Strauss and Horst W. Drescher, 547–57.
Orkneyinga saga. In Finnbogi Guðmundsson, ed., 1965, 1–300.
Scott, Sir Walter [1822] 1996. *The Pirate.* With a foreword by Andrew Wawn.
Seabrook, Mike 1994. *Max: The Life and Music of Peter Maxwell Davies.*
Taylor, Alexander Burt, trans., 1938. *The Orkneyinga Saga: A New Translation with Introduction and Notes.*
Thomson, William P. L. 2003. 'St Magnus: An Exploration of his Sainthood'. In *Stones, Skalds and Saints: The Faces of Orkney.* Ed. Doreen J. Waugh, 46–64.
Townsend, J. A. B. 1992. 'The Viking Society: A Centenary History'. *Saga-Book* 23, 180–212.

OLD NORSE MADE NEW: PAST AND PRESENT IN MODERN CHILDREN'S LITERATURE

DAVID CLARK

The academic analysis of children's literature is associated with various problems.[1] In the third edition of the critical collection *Only Connect: Readings on Children's Literature*, Peter Hunt questions the very existence of the genre of the children's book, quoting Marcus Crouch's opinion that 'there *are* no children's books' (Hunt 1996, 2; his emphasis). After a discussion in which he evaluates the process of definition itself and then how to define literature, the child, and children's literature, he comes uneasily to a definition of the last as 'books read by, especially suitable for, or especially satisfying for, members of the group currently defined by children', an accommodating definition, but one of limited practical use, as he admits (Hunt 1996, 15). The remit of the genre is not its only problem; many of the books it includes are of a popular and ephemeral nature, and this causes the editors of *Only Connect* to remark that where children's literature is concerned, 'overview articles are almost passé' (Egoff et al. 1996, xiv). Hundreds, even thousands, of new titles are produced every year, many of which quickly go out of print, and so general surveys of the field are impractical and of limited use. It is perhaps this element of transience which led to a third problem associated until comparatively recently with children's books: a lack of status within the academy. In her article on the critical reading of children's books, Julia Briggs remarks on the neglect of the academic study of children's literature, particularly in the United Kingdom, until the 1980s when, largely in connexion with the Bodleian Library's major acquisition of the Opie Collection and the University of Oxford's series of public lectures, efforts were made to have children's literature recognized in this country as a legitimate field of research (Briggs 1996, 19, 29–30). Nevertheless, an academic snobbery about children's literature, as about (and perhaps connected to) fantasy literature and science fiction, persists in certain circles.[2]

---

[1] Recent overviews of and critical collections on children's literature include Hunt 1990, 1992, 2001, and 2004, Lesnik-Oberstein 2004, Rudd 2004, Sarland 2004.

[2] Further problems associated with children's literature and the relation of adult to child, and of both to the children's book, are explored in Rose 1992 and Lesnik-Oberstein 1994.

However, more recently it has been recognized that as well as being legitimate objects of research in their own right, children's books are particularly interesting in terms of the cultural work that they perform and what this can reveal about their implied audience and its anxieties and concerns (see further, passim, Egoff et al. 1996). Like fantasy, children's literature can ask 'What if?'—that is, it can explore unasked or unanswered questions and possibilities; it can work through the commonly felt need to belong and have a place and a purpose; it can investigate issues of empowerment, good versus evil, right versus power or authority, personal struggle and how one can transcend or cope with that struggle. Additionally, it often explores notions such as the idea that magic and special gifts come with associated problems (while they solve other problems like boredom, feeling alone or different), or that one needs to adapt to the situations in which one finds oneself whilst simultaneously needing to discover and maintain a sense of self, and to find a place where that self can feel fulfilled and appreciated.

After outlining the definition of children's literature quoted above, Hunt goes on to argue for a distinction between children's books which 'are essentially contemporary' (that is, those which are still read by children) and 'historical children's books' (older or outdated works which are now more often read by reminiscing adults or by academics studying the genre than by children themselves). The present essay, then, is somewhat paradoxical, in that it observes this distinction between the past and present in terms of the period of writing, but simultaneously explores the present's rewriting and appropriation of the past. This essay is particularly interested in books in which, in exploring the issues and themes outlined above, the Norse past affects or invades the present, as will be explained shortly. It sprang from the basic question: why might a children's writer want to take Old Norse culture or literature as his or her inspiration? Various answers to this question are possible on more or less complex levels, and naturally more than one motivation may coexist. Nevertheless, such answers provide material for at least a partial discussion and analysis of wider trends in the modern reception of Old Norse and what this may reveal about contemporary perceptions of the Viking and Scandinavian past. There are far too many children's books which make reference to, or use, Norse motifs and material to discuss them comprehensively or definitively here, and so this essay concentrates in detail on just a few individual works.

In considering an author's possible reasons for writing children's literature in the first place, one may assume that the primary motivation is not merely a financial one, since (Harry Potter and Mysterious Incidents aside) it is not the most lucrative field a mercenary author could choose. However, commercial concerns are certainly one potential reason for using Norse motifs within that field. The stereotyped image of the Vikings as violent but exciting barbarians is an attractive one, as shown by the popularity of *Vicious Vikings*, Terry Deary's Norse contribution to the Horrible Histories books, which capitalize on the sensational and gory elements of the past (Deary 1994).

A subtler form of commercialism is seen in what might be termed 'exploitation novels'—that is, novels which use Norse mythic motifs or Scandinavian names or merely the stereotyped image of the Vikings as a sort of colouring or semiotic shorthand, without really engaging with the original material in any meaningful way. For instance, *Odin's Voice* by Susan Price is set in a sort of 'cod' medieval future, where society is divided into freemen and freewomen on the one hand and 'bonders' on the other, but there is a colony on Mars and technology is advanced enough to let a freeperson genetically modify his or her hair with jellyfish genes to change colour according to the owner's mood. The society is pluralistic, everyone believing comfortably in his or her own god, with the temple of Apollo next to that of Odin, and personal names like 'Affrodite' and 'Thorsgift' coexisting with 'Kylie' (Price 2005).

What is disappointing, however, is that there is actually very little use made of Norse material. The book begins promisingly, as we listen in on a shamanistic trance and a bonder girl prophesies the future. At this point there are the obligatory details of how Odin lost his eye to gain wisdom, and an interesting description of him as 'the shifty, deceitful God' who betrays those who trust him, a characterization which fits in well with the eddic depictions (cf. *Grímnismál* and Larrington's comment in Larrington 1996, 50). However, it quickly becomes apparent that the Norse elements merely provide colour for a run-of-the-mill sci-fi fantasy novel. Rather than exploring genuine medieval social categories, 'bonder' and 'freeman' are merely convenient labels for rich and poor, and there is almost no genuine engagement with Norse myth here.

Nevertheless, in general what one might call Norse-ploitation seems to be more characteristic of the adult market, where a sensationalized version of Norse culture can provide a colourful setting on which to hang a journeyman plot, as with the decidedly adult novel *Shadow of the Wolf* by Robert Holdstock (advisedly hiding under the pseudonym Chris Carlsen). This novel, which even the author regards as shameful, applies Conan the Barbarian's principles of pornographic violence to other aspects of the so-called Dark Ages, and explores the more lurid and seedy possibilities of the berserker trope (Carlsen 1977a).[3]

A rather more nuanced appropriation of Norse material comes in Robert Westall's novel *The Wind Eye*, published in 1976. It is a book mainly concerned with the supernatural interaction of St Cuthbert and seventh-century Northumbria with a troubled mid-twentieth-century family. However, there are some important Norse-related motifs in the novel. The first is the use of the Vikings who attacked Lindisfarne as a means of emphasizing Westall's thematic exploration of violence. The boy character Michael in chapter 6 is shown having a fight with his father Bertrand, an amusingly sour caricature of an academic, who has been pontificating to his children on the Viking names of the Farne Islands. Michael deliberately tries to annoy his father by saying 'Bet the Vikings thumped hell out of the monks.' Westall continues:

> Bertrand winced at such crudeness; then controlled himself and said, 'Yes, the Vikings burnt Holy Island twice; in A.D. 793 and again in 875.'
> 'Murderous bastards,' said Mike appreciatively.
> 'That's a rather imprecise way of seeing it,' said Bertrand coldly. 'There was certainly a conflict of cultures, but it's too easy to condemn the Vikings as mere villains. They were, after all, obeying their own ethical code. Doing their own thing, as you would say. They were superb navigators, discovered America five hundred years before Columbus, and their wood-carving is magnificent. They weren't just thugs.'
> 'Bet old Cuddy wouldn't have agreed with you,' said Mike. 'Not when he saw them burning *his* monastery.' (Westall 1976, 33)

The historical violence associated with the Vikings (sometimes unfairly, as Bertrand points out) serves here to bring out the latent violence of the father-son relationship.

An actual Viking attack on Lindisfarne features later in the novel when the children find an old boat aptly called the Resurrection. They sail out to sea in it and suddenly find they are no longer in the present, but have somehow returned to the seventh century and to the time of Cuthbert, whom the locals know as the Wind Eye of the novel's title.

---

[3] *Shadow of the Wolf* is the first in the *Berserker Trilogy*, a rebirth cycle in which each time the 'hero' dies he is reborn into an earlier era, retreating from the era of the Norse raids into an Arthurian fifth century (Carlsen 1977b) and then Roman Britain at the time of Boudicca's uprising (Carlsen 1979). In an interview with Raymond H. Thompson, Holdstock admits that these were 'hack books', and that he is 'very ashamed' of 'the violence and the appalling misogyny' of these early works (Thompson 1989).

This name is explained towards the end of the book in a nice passage in which a character gives the etymology of the word 'window'—'Derived from Icelandic *vindr* meaning wind and *auga* meaning eye [...]. The old Norse for *window* is *wind eye*' (Westall 1976, 154). St Cuthbert is thus envisioned in the novel as a kind of window or portal enabling the child and adult characters to see—not from inside to outside, but from the present to the past, and to see themselves and others with more insight.

What is significant about the Viking attack, though, is that it is not just described as a violent raid of murderous Vikings upon innocent monks, although that element is certainly present. First of all, there is an explicit recognition of the element of myth-making in the usual presentation of Vikings—that, as Westall says, 'huge figures with wings on their helmets, and great flowing beards [only exist in] Victorian history-books' (Westall 1976, 137). The novel's description of the raiders is much more realistic—they are a bunch of short, badly-organized smelly bullies, whose swords are dented and rusty: 'Like a mob of Irish tinkers dressed up badly for a fancy-dress ball.'

Westall's treatment of violence is more nuanced than this, however. At various points throughout the novel, he shows the violence of emotionally manipulative behaviour, or of the use of superior intelligence to wound and belittle. As a result of his interaction with Saint Cuthbert, the father character, Bertrand, repents of his own intellectual aggression and intolerance, which he has realized masks or displaces an impulse toward the physical violence which he condemns and despises in others.

There is a more than slightly anti-academic element to the novel, suggesting that Westall perceives a nasty edge to (at least the public side of) academia. For instance, the passage where Bertrand's son Mike rather unfairly tries to explain him to his sister, who has been upset by their father's appalling behaviour:

> You know how he can't stand being proved wrong. Don't you remember the time the Oxford bloke attacked him in the *Observer*? He was just like this—until he'd written that book to prove the bloke wrong. He's O.K., Bertrand—till somebody stubs him out, and then he turns into a bloody sadistic maniac. (Westall 1976, 105)

In fact, there is a sense at the very end of the novel that Bertrand has been converted from an academic into something more meaningful. He decides to resign his fellowship and comb the shores of the Farne Islands for evidence of Cuthbert and study the objects he finds, with the eventual aim of being able to sail back on the Resurrection and, as he puts it, 'someday, somehow, slip through the time-curtain again and meet Cuddy face-to-face and never return to the dry-as-dust twentieth century' (Westall 1976, 156–57). In the context of the novel as a whole, this is an interesting association between a materialistic twentieth century, overly obsessed with science and rational explanations, and the activity of the scholar, studying history and the past, but not being able to see its point, and indeed hiding from it. Westall, in his Author's Note, speaks of exploring the 'relationship between truth, belief and legend' (Westall 1976, 159), and, presumably, in this semi-historical, semi-contemporary novel Westall sees himself as not only making the past live, but also showing that past and present are inextricably linked and intertwined and influence each other.

I want to explore the relation of past and present in more detail shortly, through various types of what may loosely be called 'historical novels'. However, first I want to look at modern retellings or reworkings of medieval Norse texts, to introduce a theory or methodology which I hope to show can be applied productively to other Norse-influenced texts.

In terms of what one might think of as straightforward 'retellings' of the Norse myths, there is, I think, an instructive difference between modern retellings and the kind produced in the Victorian and Edwardian periods. One thinks of the many reprints of Annie and Eliza Keary's *The Heroes of Asgard*. This book was first produced in 1857 with the longer title *The Heroes of Asgard and the Giants of Jotunheim; or, The Week and Its Story* and was set within a frame narrative which was omitted in subsequent editions (Keary 1857 and 1870). It quickly became popular as a schoolbook, and it is in fact still in print with Dover Publications (Keary 2005). The book contains stories with 'Just So' titles such as 'How Thor Went to Jotunheim', 'The Wanderings of Freyja', and 'The Punishment of Loki', and it is very much in line with nineteenth- and early twentieth-century approaches to mythology for children—to tell bowdlerized versions of the stories in a simple and elegant style, to interleave the texts with beautiful plates in brown or grey tone, and to make the books to all intents and purposes homogeneous with retellings of any other set of myths, whether Roman, Greek, Celtic, or Babylonian. One might compare the thick uniform multi-set volumes one still finds thronging second-hand bookshops with series titles like 'Told Through the Ages', or 'Myth and Legend in Literature and Art', where *Legends of Ancient Egypt* sits alongside *Told By the Northmen: Stories from the Eddas and Sagas*, and *Myths and Legends of Babylonia and Assyria* accompanies *Myths of the Norsemen* (Brooksbank 1923, Wilmot-Buxton 1903; Spence 1916, Guerber 1908). One finds a concerted effort to tone down or absorb anything alien or potentially upsetting in the original, presumably reflecting a desire to educate but not to disturb children. Some of them are nevertheless beautiful in both style and visual appearance, and can still have a huge imaginative impact on children.

In more recent times, one finds a rather more sophisticated approach to retelling, for instance, in Kevin Crossley-Holland's *Axe-Age, Wolf-Age*, first published in 1985. Again one finds stories interspersed with illustrations, but these versions are much closer to the originals, and less keen to derive bourgeois morals from them. Crossley-Holland is clearly anxious to foreground his awareness that he is adding or reworking. In his Foreword he says that he has closely followed the *Prose* and *Poetic Eddas*, but 'did not hesitate to develop hints, flesh out dramatic situations and add snatches of dialogue' (Crossley-Holland 1985, 13). He also says he has used other sources to provide what he calls a 'descriptive background' to the myths. What is interesting, however, is that he feels the need to take two further actions: first, to use 'good, blunt words with Anglo-Saxon roots whenever I could do so.' This clearly proceeds from the popular association of Anglo-Saxon elements in English with straightforward, frank bluntness, as opposed to Latin and French elements deemed to be more sophisticated and polysyllabic. But it also makes an interesting link between Anglo-Saxon and Norse cultures— there is a sense that it is appropriate to retell Norse stories in a language that emphasizes its Anglo-Saxon elements, and perhaps that this somehow helps an English audience to appropriate the Norse myths as part of their own heritage. The second decision, however, which is editorial in nature, is to order the myths in such a way as to provide 'a psychologically satisfying sequence, leading inescapably toward Ragnarok' and to reduce 'contradictions and chronological inconsistencies to a minimum.' Crossley-Holland is well aware of the multifarious origins of the Norse myths and that a unified mythology is itself a myth, but feels the need to create for a modern audience a metanarrative which unifies and gives consistency to these myths.

There is an interesting tension between the process of familiarization he describes here, and his implicit justification for retelling these myths earlier in the Foreword. There he seems at first to validate the *unfamiliar*: the Norse myths which describe creation or reveal how the world works, he says, 'provide explanations which enable us to see the old world around us with new eyes' (Crossley-Holland 1985, 12). Here, it may be helpful to invoke the theory of 'defamiliarization', which the formalist critic Shklovsky defines and sees as integral to literature. He states:

After we see an object several times, we begin to recognize it. The object is in front of us and we know about it, but we do not see it—hence we cannot say anything significant about it. Art removes objects from the automatism of perception (Shklovsky 1988, 21).

Although he is perhaps one of the first theorists to see literature as primarily defined by this process, Shklovsky is, of course, not the first writer to be aware of or explore the concept of 'making strange'.[4] An often-cited example of the process is the riddle, where an object or concept may be described from an unusual perspective with the intention not merely of confusing the audience, but of challenging them to see the thing described in a new way.[5] However, Shklovsky provides a convenient term for and theorization of the process and a place from which to begin to explore it further within the present context.

After invoking this trope (consciously or unconsciously), Crossley-Holland goes on to talk about what the myths tell us of the people who created them: 'their spirit and confidence and wit, [. . .] their cunning and ruthlessness and fatalism' (Crossley-Holland 1985, 12). But he immediately seeks to counter any impression that the myths are not therefore relevant to the twentieth century:

> like all great imaginative literature, the myths are not imprisoned in their own time and place; they tell us of their makers but they also tell us a lot about ourselves—our own deep longings and fears.

We shall return shortly to this concept of a dual attitude that myths are both familiar and unfamiliar, and that their familiar elements can serve paradoxically to defamiliarize things we take for granted and thus are blind to.[6]

First, however, we shall consider a text which is perhaps more a reworking than a retelling of a Norse text, the recent novel by Melvin Burgess, *Bloodtide* (Burgess 1999a), which recasts *Vǫlsunga saga* as a bloody story of gangland feuds, genetically-modified human-animals, murder, rape and incest, set in a post-apocalyptic London and the surrounding Wasteland. Burgess is the controversial author who brought

---

[4] The English translation 'defamiliarization' renders the Russian word *ostranenie*, literally, 'making strange'.

[5] On this process in the Old English riddle (although he does not explicitly use the term defamiliarization), see Smith 2000, especially 80.

[6] One might compare with Crossley-Holland's methodology Isabel Wyatt's *Thorkill of Iceland*, which uses compounding, word-formation, and other techniques to recreate a 'saga style' in which to retell stories reminiscent of the more episodic legendary sagas (Wyatt 1997).

drug-abuse and underage sex to the world of children's literature in books such as *Junk* and *Doing It* (Burgess 1999b and 2003). He himself describes *Bloodtide* on his website in the following terms:

> Set in a decaying, futuristic London taken over by gang-law, it is a tragic story of love and hate, revenge and destiny. Described as repulsive, compulsive, disgusting and classic, its imagery is drawn from computer games, film and comics, and the story itself from the ancient Icelandic Volsunga saga. (Burgess 2006)

Burgess is clearly keen to emphasize the sensational and up-to-date elements of his novel, but, although he implies that they stem from the influence of contemporary media, the reader of his medieval source knows that the inference that *Vǫlsunga saga* provided plot only is disingenuous. In *Bloodtide*, the bloodthirsty Volsung clan transform quite successfully into London *mafiosi* who hang the corpses of their enemies in a disused lift which spans their vast multi-storey skyscraper. There is a wry humour in Burgess's account of the Volsungs' attempt to hang the 'hanging-god' Odin, which of course turns out to have unforeseen and dire consequences. What is fascinating is the way that the weird post-apocalyptic scenes and grotesque array of deformed or geneticallymodified characters provide a rationale for several elements of the original story which one would expect otherwise to jar in a modern setting, such as the corporeal appearance of a god, or a knife that can cut through stone but then only be withdrawn again by Burgess's version of Sigmundr, or men who turn out to be werewolves. The novel follows the plot of the original saga extremely closely, and in many ways it also captures the amoral elements of the original too.[7] These are dark and bloody books, but their popularity and their promise to win popularity for their Norse sources is witnessed to by Cordelia, 'aged 17', who says on the inside of the cover of *Bloodtide*: 'This was a really good book! Imaginative, intense and clever . . . Gruesome and gory, but so were the old myths.'

In *The Wind Eye*, Westall uses the image of the Vikings to explore the themes of violence and the interaction of past and present in his novel. Crossley-Holland's collection tries to create an 'Anglo-Saxon' Norse

---

[7] *Bloodsong* (Burgess 2005) continues the story and contains even more (perhaps overly) ingenious futuristic matches for the original elements (particularly the forgetfulness potion motif), but the narrator is more intrusive and the style less sure, at least at the beginning of the novel. There is ample material for a fuller study of *Bloodtide* and its sequel *Bloodsong*. For a brief consideration of *Bloodtide* and *Bloodsong* in relation to *Vǫlsunga saga*, see O'Donoghue 2007, 190–95.

mythology which makes the past familiar and defamiliarizes the present. Burgess recasts a medieval Norse text as a futuristic novel which preserves many elements of the contents and quality of his original. All three engage imaginatively not only with Norse material but also with the implications of what they are doing and the relation of past and present. The genre which performs this kind of work *par excellence* is, of course, the historical novel, and the rest of this essay is concerned with this genre, loosely conceived.

The traditional historical novel will not receive extended consideration here, although its existence cannot be ignored.[8] There are of course many children's novels based in medieval Scandinavia, or around Viking or Norse characters (often seen through the eyes of children themselves). The most famous of these writers (and justly so) are Henry Treece and Rosemary Sutcliff. Each of them wrote many historical novels set in various periods, including several which touch on Viking or Scandinavian characters and events. Most notable perhaps are Treece's Viking trilogy, written between 1955 and 1960, and Sutcliff's *The Shield Ring*, *Blood Feud*, and *Sword Song*, the first written in 1956 about the Viking defence against the Norman conquerors in the Lake District, the second in 1976 about an English boy sold as a slave to the Northmen, the third in 1997 about the adventures of a boy banished from a Viking settlement in north-eastern England (Treece 1955, 1957 and 1960, Sutcliff 1976 and 1999). A recent example of this genre is Nancy Farmer's novel *The Sea of Trolls* (although it adds heavy fantasy elements to its reimagining of the historical past; Farmer 2004).[9] These books are perennially popular and the complex relation of their contents to the historical past, and what this indicates about their implied audience, would repay extended discussion. Some of these texts try to encourage contemporary moral virtues, mediated by the distancing effect of the historical setting. For instance, Molly Holden's *The Unfinished Feud* takes the familiar saga plot of a feud between families and uses the protagonist to show (rather heavy-handedly) how a courageous individual can bring an end to the cycle of revenge (Holden 1970). The publication of this book at

---

[8] For an overview of the genre with reference to children's literature, see Fisher 2004. For earlier historical fiction, see McGarry and White 1963 (especially sections II.A.1.b.3 and II.A.2.b.3).

[9] Notable too is Pauline Clarke's *Torolv the Fatherless*, which retells and contextualizes the story of the Battle of Maldon (Clarke 1959). See Mary Moffat's online annotated bibliography for further examples and discussion (Moffat 2006), and Hotchkiss 1972, 22–26.

the beginning of the 1970s, after Vietnam and during the *détente* period of the Cold War, might suggest the motivation for this work. On the other hand, texts such as Treece's and Sutcliff's seem to delight in exploring the past for its own sake, along with the differences of the way of life of medieval children from that of their contemporary readers; they perform a delicate balancing act between (meticulously researched) historical authenticity and the exploration of recurring themes of childhood.[10] In fact, child characters seem ideally placed to function as mediators for the historical novelist—not yet adult, not fully part of society, they can both provide a link to their modern counterpart and a relative outsider's perspective on their culture and society. Much further work remains to be done in this area, and particularly interesting would be a comparative discussion of the cultural work performed by historical novels aimed at the adult market, such as those by Bernard Cornwell, whose *Saxon Stories* tell the story of Alfred the Great through the eyes of an English boy captured and adopted by the Danes (Cornwell 2004, 2005, and 2006), or Tim Severin, whose *Viking* series recounts the travels and adventures of Thorgils, son of Leif the Lucky (Severin 2005). However, the number of these texts is such that an overview would be impractical here, and, moreover, this essay is less concerned with attempts to recreate Norse history and culture than with exploring literary uses of that history or culture in other contexts, and specifically in texts in which the past invades the present.

Linda Hall has characterized such texts as one form of the 'time-slip story', tracing this sub-genre back to 1906 and the publication of Rudyard Kipling's *Puck of Pook's Hill* and Edith Nesbit's *The Story of the Amulet*, and including in the tradition authors such as Lucy M. Boston, Penelope Lively, Philippa Pearce, and Alison Uttley (Hall 2001, 43–45).[11] However, Laura Smith's sub-genre of the 'domestic fantasy', which introduces 'a touch of magic' into 'a realistic setting within a realistic family', is also helpful for the two texts discussed below (Smith 2004, 447). As an example from adult fiction one might adduce Tom Holt's famous 1988 comic novel *Who's Afraid of Beowulf?* which resurrects King Hrólfr

---

[10] On Sutcliff, see further Spenser 1965, and the author's own comments on her work in Sutcliff 2001; on Treece, see Clarke 1966.

[11] Unlike traditional historical novels, which are squarely set in the past (as with Treece and Sutcliff), 'time-slip' novels make characters from the present invade the past (Uttley, Nesbit), or the past invade the present (as with the novels discussed in the following sections), or explore a complex interaction of past and present (as with Boston, Pearce, or Westall). See further Hall 2001.

kraki and Ǫrvar-Oddr, and in which the medieval and the modern collide in a very amusing but thoughtful dynamic (Holt 1988) or, with a wider mythological remit, Neil Gaiman's recent *American Gods* (2001). Here, specifically, I want to look in detail at two children's books in which characters and events from Old Norse mythology invade modern reality.

The first is *Warriors of the Raven*, published in 2001 as the final part of a trilogy by Alan Gibbons. Here, Norse myth enters the computer age, as part of a—not Virtual Reality but—Parallel Reality computer game where the players enter the world of the Norse gods (Gibbons 2001, 9). However, it quickly becomes clear that this process is not just about bringing Norse myth alive and allowing children to become vicarious heroes. In this book, something utterly Other is trying in the form of Loki to enter human reality *through* human myths and stories, and it has selected Norse myth for what it thinks is the final battle because, as it says, it is a mythology 'Where man and god are both mortal. Where the power of Evil can triumph' (118). Details from the story of Ragnarǫk are skilfully and accurately woven into the narrative, and the perception of the Norse world as gloomy and pessimistic clearly parallels the author's depiction of the real world. The audience is given a conventional binary choice between good and evil, and moralizing comments about the monster inside us all, but the ending of the novel is far from facile. There is no guarantee that good will win, there are fatal consequences to failure, and both storytelling and technology are presented as addictive, seductive media with the power to draw children into a dangerous adult world, where playing the game and entering the myth (whether imaginatively or physically) can lead to mental and even physical destruction (Gibbons 2001, 11, 148). Even the hero in this book, a fourteen-year-old boy portentously named Phoenix, defeats Loki only temporarily, and the price he pays is to be cut off from his human existence, family, and friends, and to be endlessly reborn in a world where every myth, dream, and legend exists (Gibbons 2001, 164–66). That heroism demands sacrifice is a literary commonplace, but it is less common in children's literature to find the notion that a child might not only *feel* he or she does not belong, but perhaps really does not belong in this world at all.

The final text to be considered here is Diana Wynne Jones's book, *Eight Days of Luke*, which was originally written in 1975, but is still in print, and remains popular with both children and adults (Jones 1975).[12]

---

[12] For another account of *Eight Days of Luke*, in the context of a discussion of the concept of the 'double audience' (one knowledgeable, the other ignorant about the Norse influences behind a work), see O'Donoghue 2007, 190–95.

The novel is told from the perspective of its central character, a fourteen-year-old boy named David. David's parents are both dead and he dreads the school holidays because he has to stay with his Great Aunt and Uncle and his cousins, all of whom are obnoxious in different ways and all of whom blame David for everything and continually try to make him feel guilty for not expressing enough gratitude to them for allowing him to exist (Jones 1975, 9–10, 99–100). One day, however, David is so angry at the constant injustice that he begins to invent curses in a made-up language. Suddenly the ground shakes and opens, snakes start to slither out, and a strange boy appears who calls himself Luke and seems to think that David has saved him from a dreadful prison (Jones 1975, 33–40). The book's trajectory is clear from here on. Luke is evidently the Norse god Loki. Rather strangely he is continually associated with fire, which seems to be Jones's conflation of Loki with Logi, the personification of flame Snorri describes during his account of the tricking of Þórr in *Gylfaginning* (Jones 1975, 43, 61, 65).[13] The rest of the Æsir turn up at David's house looking for Loki, appropriately on the days of the week which are named after them, so a character called Mr Chew turns up on Tuesday, Mr Wedding turns up on Wednesday, Mr and Mrs Fry turn up on Friday.[14]

What is interesting in the present context is the way that Jones, like the other authors considered above, both familiarizes and defamiliarizes by this narrative process. Óðinn (or Mr Wedding) now has a 'posh' car driven by a lady chauffeur, instead of the horse Sleipnir and a valkyrie, and he talks to David in terms which are rather strange for a modern-day adult, but which are very reminiscent of *Hávamál*—for instance when he talks of the laws of hospitality (Jones 1975, 99–100). In this same scene, while David is looking at Wedding, he suddenly notices that he only has one eye, although he had clearly had two before. We are told that David senses somehow that this is Wedding's 'true face, and his real nature' (Jones 1975, 104). Jones seems to suggest a dynamic where the gods can manifest themselves in various ways in different periods or contexts, but that this is just a mask, that their true nature lies behind: something that cannot be fully assimilated to modern life.

---

[13] O'Donoghue argues that Jones is here modelling Luke on Wagner's Loge (O'Donoghue 2007, 194–95), although Jones has expressed her dislike of and desire to break free from the influence of Wagner's *Der Ring des Nibelungen* (Jones, personal communication).

[14] The gods' names thus appear in their Anglo-Saxon forms, although they are clearly based on the Norse accounts of their attributes and history.

Jones also exhibits in *Eight Days of Luke*, though, a clear desire to find the appropriate equivalent from modern life for Norse motifs, as for instance when David goes to see Sigurðr and his *einheriar*, here refigured as a crew of teenage bikers in leather jackets and tattoos playing pinball machines in a men-only club (Jones 1975, 175). There are various other elements of Norse mythology that Jones aptly and entertainingly conveys. However, it is the changes that Jones makes which are perhaps more interesting, and the most important of these is her refiguring of Loki. Her Luke is someone who at first seems to be a sixteen-year-old boy with family problems. When David expresses annoyance early on at his family going on at him all the time, Luke sympathizes, saying: 'Oh, I know what that feels like [. . .]. My family was just the same' (Jones 1975, 52). Later Luke claims that he has no idea what he did to be tied up with snakes dripping poison on him, rather he says: 'Somebody did something, and they blamed it on me [. . .]. They always blame it on me' (Jones 1975, 117). And when David replies: 'Just like they blame me', the unmotivatedly malevolent Loki of *Gylfaginning* or *Warriors of the Raven* suddenly becomes a hard-done-by boy from an unreasonable and troubled family.

This manipulation of her material fits into the rationale that Jones herself intelligently describes for the novel. She is clearly far from the unacademic writer she often portrays herself as being. For instance, in an email to me she claimed that she could not remember any of her sources for the Old Norse material in *Luke*, that it all came from childhood memories (Jones, personal communication). This may well be true, but elsewhere Jones is clearly well aware of what she is doing when she makes use of medieval material, as one might expect of the wife of the distinguished medievalist John Burrow, and someone who attended the lectures of Lewis and Tolkien as an Oxford undergraduate in the 1950s.

In her essay 'Inventing the Middle Ages' Jones amply demonstrates her wide and careful reading in medieval literature, particularly Middle English, and she also makes a couple of significant comments about *Eight Days of Luke*. These comments come in the context of a discussion of the medieval idea of what she calls 'story-time'—the concept that whatever time stories come from, it is 'conceived as being contemporary with their own', for instance, the way that *Troilus and Criseyde* contains a mixture of historical details and elements more appropriate to fourteenth-century England (Jones 1997). Jones comments:

> I took this idea up with enthusiasm. It is why most of what I write is set in this modern age whenever possible. For instance, writing an early book called

Eight Days of Luke [. . .] I was quite consciously imitating what I took to be a medieval treatment of 'story-time'.

However, in common with the dynamic outlined earlier with regard to Crossley-Holland's collection, Jones's remarks on her work show a tension between the desires to familiarize and to defamiliarize. Indeed, she sees her role as a sort of translator of stories, quite akin to Crossley-Holland's. She goes on in 'Inventing the Middle Ages' to discuss various ways to write about different situations, including the following:

> [Do you want to write about] a boy struggling into adolescence in the face of an unkind family? Have the boy's feelings appear in the shape of the Norse gods. But in all these instances you must not cheat. You must have the magical occurrences strongly effective in their own terms—they must leave their mark on the everyday life of the characters in the story. (Jones 1997)

In contrast, in her essay on 'Heroes', Jones says that *Eight Days of Luke* sprang out of her fascination with the fact that we daily talk about the days of the week using the names of the Germanic gods. As she says,

> just as Woden's Day and Thor's Day are part of our everyday lives, so are the big things for which these gods stand. And we respond to them as people always have done. (Jones 1992)

This idea of the interconnectedness of the extraordinary and the everyday is exemplified in the scene when David goes to seek counsel of the three Norns, next to Mímir's Well and the World-Tree. When one of the Norns takes their single shared eye out of her eye socket, we are given the following description of it from David's perspective:

> It came out rather more easily than Astrid's contact-lenses and in much the same way. Alan, who had never seen Astrid take a lens out, looked sick. (Jones 1975, 162)

This comparison is not only very apt and designed to delight children with its combination of the familiar and the squeamish, but it also encapsulates the idea that one needs a link to the familiar, a 'hook', in order to be able to understand a new concept: an author needs to invoke a world-view onto which the new concept can be mapped. On a larger level than detachable eyes, the Norse gods are explicable to the children's audience via the familiar scenario of a misunderstood teenager with an unreasonable family, but the Norse gods also allow the issues and situation of a misunderstood teenager to be worked through at a slight distance and from a different perspective.

The desire to re-familiarize the past and the hidden thus coexists with the desire to defamiliarize modern situations by the shock of the past or the mythic entering the present. In *Eight Days of Luke* this dynamic may connect to Jones's avowed dislike of unhappy endings. In one of her interviews she describes worrying away at how to come out with a happy ending, talking in terms of problem-solving, even of a 'Eureka' moment when she finds the solution (Rosenberg 2002, 67, 168). It is, of course, the common understanding that if one steps outside a problem and distances oneself from it, one can often solve or resolve it—to solve the Exeter Book Riddles, for instance, certainly takes lateral thinking. And this concept seems to work with *Eight Days of Luke*—the defamiliarizing elements of the Norse gods' interaction with modern life allow the main character's problematic situation to be resolved. David's intervention in Luke's troubled family situation is paralleled by Mr Wedding's intervention in David's life, which results in the promise of a happy family dynamic (199–200). It is a much more positive slant on childhood than we saw in Gibbons' *Warriors of the Raven*, reflecting the earlier period at which Jones wrote the novel but also her personal philosophy as an author.

The concepts of familiarization and defamiliarization are, of course, not unique either to Old Norse literature or to children's literature. However, I would like finally to examine the idea that they are particularly appropriate to both in conjunction with one another. Old Norse as one of many past cultures and literatures raises the much-debated question for a modern devotee, whether editor, translator, or adapter: how does one best reproduce or represent past texts or world-views? Edward Irving sees the issue in these terms:

> do we present the poem as *Then*, stressing its alien condition, embedded as it is in a remote time, or do we present it as *Now*, trying to bring out its still living qualities as a still possible experience for today's reader? (Irving 1998, 14)

Irving is writing on the editing of Old English poetry, but his remarks are equally applicable to translation, or film adaptation. One answer to Irving's question is that a balance between both needs to be achieved, as was argued with regard to Sutcliff above. In terms of texts aimed at the general public, the Norse in the guise of Vikings are familiar from childhood, but only in a stereotyped or at least limited version of the historical reality, and an author needs to capitalize on the audience's familiarity whilst ideally extending its understanding and making it more nuanced: essentially to balance familiar with unfamiliar aspects. The idea of defamiliarization is also commonly associated with children in our culture—that is, the idea that children are unfamiliar with things that we take for granted, but also that their fresh and naïve perspective can often result in us seeing these things from a new angle or discovering new aspects of them. Certainly, it is frequently employed as a narrative technique in modern children's literature. Since Old Norse material on the one hand demands both cultural and linguistic translation, and on the other hand often seems particularly exotic and contains elements perennially popular with children, it is perhaps unsurprising that authors who work with it have been particularly thoughtful about the balance of the familiar and the unfamiliar necessary in representing it to a modern audience. It will be interesting to see how the use of Norse material develops over the next decades, but what is certain is that authors' intellectual and imaginative engagement with Norse mythology, culture, and literature will continue to draw children and adults alike back to the sources of their inspiration, and that Old Norse will continue to inspire the desire to 'make it new'.

Bibliography

Ben-Amos, Daniel 1976. 'Analytical Categories and Ethnic Genres'. In *Folklore Genres*. Ed. Daniel Ben-Amos. Publications of the American Folklore Society, Bibliographical and Special Series 26, 215–42.

Briggs, Julia 1996. 'Critical Opinion: Reading Children's Books'. In Egoff et al. 1996, 18–31.

Brooksbank, F. H. 1923. *Legends of Ancient Egypt: Stories of Egyptian Gods and Heroes*. Illustrated by Evelyn Paul.

Burgess, Melvin 1999a. *Bloodtide*.

Burgess, Melvin 1999b. *Junk*.

Burgess, Melvin 2003. *Doing It*.

Burgess, Melvin 2005. *Bloodsong*.

Burgess, Melvin 2006. http://web.onetel.net.uk/~melvinburgess/bookspage.1.htm

Carlsen, Chris 1977a. *Shadow of the Wolf*. Berserker Trilogy 1.

Carlsen, Chris 1977b. *The Bull Chief*. Berserker Trilogy 2.

Carlsen, Chris 1979. *The Horned Warrior*. Berserker Trilogy 3.

Clarke, Pauline 1959. *Torolv the Fatherless*.

Clarke, Pauline 1966. 'Henry Treece: Lament for a Maker'. In *The Times Literary Supplement* Thursday November 24, 1966, 1072 (anonymous review). Repr. in Egoff et al. 1969, 256–64.

Collins, Fiona M. and Judith Graham, eds, 2001. *Historical Fiction for Children: Capturing the Past*.

Cornwell, Bernard 2004. *The Last Kingdom*.

Cornwell, Bernard 2005. *The Pale Horseman*.

Cornwell, Bernard 2006. *The Lords of the North*.

Crossley-Holland, Kevin 1985. *Axe-Age, Wolf-Age: A Selection from the Norse Myths*.

Deary, Terry 1994. *Horrible Histories: The Vicious Vikings*. Illustrated by Martin Brown.

Egoff, Sheila, G. T. Stubbs, and L. F. Ashley, eds, 1969. *Only Connect: Readings on Children's Literature*. 1st edn.

Egoff, Sheila, Gordon Stubbs, Ralph Ashley, and Wendy Sutton, eds, 1996. *Only Connect: Readings on Children's Literature*. 3rd edn.

Farmer, Nancy 2004. *The Sea of Trolls*.

Fisher, Janet 2004. 'Historical Fiction'. In Hunt 2004a, I 490–98.

Gaiman, Neil 2001. *American Gods*.

Gibbons, Alan 2001. *Warriors of the Raven*.

Guerber, H. A. 1908. *Myths of the Norsemen. From the Eddas and Sagas*.

Hall, Linda 2001. '"Time No Longer"—History, Enchantment and the Classic Time-Slip Story'. In Collins and Graham 2001, 43–53.

Holden, Molly 1970. *The Unfinished Feud*.

Holt, Tom 1988. *Who's Afraid of Beowulf?*

Hotchkiss, Jeanette 1972. *European Historical Fiction and Biography for Children and Young People*. 2nd edn.

Hunt, Peter 1990. *Children's Literature: the Development of Criticism*.

Hunt, Peter, ed., 1992. *Literature for Children: Contemporary Criticism*.

Hunt, Peter 1996. 'Defining Children's Literature'. In Egoff et al. 1996, 2–17.

Hunt, Peter 2001. *Children's Literature*.

Hunt, Peter, ed., 2004a. *International Companion Encyclopedia of Children's Literature*. 2nd edn. 2 vols.

Hunt, Peter 2004b. 'The Knowledge: What Do You Need to Know to Know Children's Literature?' In *New Voices in Children's Literature Criticism*. Ed. Sebastien Chapleau, 10–18.

Irving, Edward B. Jr. 1998. 'Editing Old English Verse: The Ideal'. In *New Approaches to Editing Old English Verse*. Ed. Sarah Larrat Keefer and Katherine O'Brien O'Keeffe, 11–20.

Jones, Diana Wynne 1975. *Eight Days of Luke*.

Jones, Diana Wynne 1992. 'Heroes'. Lecture delivered in Australia, 1992. http://www.leemac.freeserve.co.uk/heroes.htm

Jones, Diana Wynne 1997. 'Inventing the Middle Ages'. Talk given at Nottingham University, 1997. http://www.leemac.freeserve.co.uk/medieval.htm

Keary, A. and E. 1857. *The Heroes of Asgard and the Giants of Jotunheim; or, The Week and Its Story*.

Keary, A. and E. 1870. *The Heroes of Asgard: Tales from Scandinavian Mythology*.

Keary, A. and E. 2005. *The Heroes of Asgard: Tales from Scandinavian Mythology*.

Kline, D. T. 2003. *Medieval Literature for Children*.

Larrington, Carolyne, trans., 1996. *The Poetic Edda*.

Lesnik-Oberstein, Karín 1994. *Children's Literature: Criticism and the Fictional Child*.

Lesnik-Oberstein, Karín, ed., 2004. *Children's Literature: New Approaches*.

McGarry, Daniel D. and Sarah Harriman White, eds, 1963. *Historical Fiction Guide*.

Moffat, Mary 2006. http://www.marysmoffat.co.uk

O'Donoghue, Heather 2007. *From Asgard to Valhalla: The Remarkable History of the Norse Myths*.

Philips, Neil 1981. *A Fine Anger: The Work of Alan Garner*.
Price, Susan 2005. *Odin's Voice*.
Rose, Jacqueline 1992. *The Case of Peter Pan: or, The Impossibility of Children's Fiction*. Rev. edn.
Rosenberg, Teya et al., eds, 2002. *Diana Wynne Jones: An Exciting and Exacting Wisdom*. Studies in Children's Literature 1.
Rudd, David 2004. 'Theorising and Theories'. In Hunt 2004a, I 29–43.
Sarland, Charles 2004. 'Critical Tradition and Ideological Positioning'. In Hunt 2004a, I 56–75.
Severin, Tim 2005. *Odinn's Child*.
Severin, Tim 2005. *Sworn Brother*.
Severin, Tim 2005. *King's Man*.
Shklovsky, Victor [1917] 1988. 'Art as Technique'. Repr. in translation in *Modern Criticism and Theory: A Reader*. Ed. David Lodge, 16–30.
Smith, D. K. 2000. 'Humor in Hiding: Laughter Between the Sheets in the Exeter Book Riddles'. In *Humour in Anglo-Saxon Literature*. Ed. Jonathan Wilcox, 79–98.
Smith, Laura 2004. 'Domestic Fantasy'. In Hunt 2004a, 447–53.
Spence, Lewis 1916. *Myths and Legends of Babylonia and Assyria*.
Spenser, Margaret 1965. 'The Search for Selfhood: the Historical Novels of Rosemary Sutcliff'. *The Times Literary Supplement* Thursday June 17, 1965, 498 (anonymous review). Repr. in Egoff et al. 1969, 249–55.
Sutcliff, Rosemary 1956. *The Shield Ring*.
Sutcliff, Rosemary 1976. *Blood Feud*.
Sutcliff, Rosemary 1999. *Sword Song*.
Sutcliff, Rosemary [1989] 2001. 'History and Time'. In Collins and Graham 2001, 109–18.
Thompson, Raymond H. 1989. 'Interview with Robert Holdstock'. Dated 'LONDON 21 MAY 1989'. *Taliesin's Successors: Interviews with Authors of Modern Arthurian Literature*. Part of the University of Rochester's *The Camelot Project*: http://www.lib.rochester.edu/camelot/intrvws/contents.htm
Todorov, Tzvetan [1970] 1973. *The Fantastic: A Structural Approach to a Literary Genre*. Trans. Richard Howard.
Treece, Henry 1955. *Viking's Dawn*.
Treece, Henry 1957. *The Road to Miklagard*.
Treece, Henry 1960. *Viking's Sunset*.
Westall, Robert 1976. *The Wind Eye*.
Wilmot-Buxton, E. M. 1903. *Told By the Northmen: Stories from the Eddas and Sagas*.
Wyatt, Isabel 1997. *Thorkill of Iceland: Viking Hero-Tales*. (Incorporating *The Dream of King Alfdan*, first published 1961.)